ATTP 3-18.12 (FM 90-4)

I0026819

Air Assault Operations

March 2011

Headquarters, Department of the Army

Published by Books Express Publishing
Books Express Publishing, 2011
ISBN 978-1-78039-978-2

Books Express publications are available from all good retail and online booksellers. For
publishing proposals and direct ordering please contact us at: info@books-express.com

Army Tactics, Techniques, and Procedures
No. 3-18.12

Headquarters
Department of the Army
Washington, DC, 1 March 2011

Air Assault Operations

Contents

Distribution Restriction: Approved for public release; distribution is unlimited.

*This manual supersedes FM 90-4, 16 March 1987.

Figures

Tables

Preface

This manual (ATTP 3-18.12) describes how brigade combat teams (BCTs) and combat aviation brigades (CABs) plan, prepare, and conduct air assault operations. It emphasizes the coordination necessary between these organizations in regards to the planning, preparation, and tactical employment of both elements.

The target audience for this manual is commanders; leaders; and staffs at brigade, battalion, and company level. However, this manual applies to other organizations that are required to plan and operate as part of an air assault task force (AATF). This manual provides these leaders with descriptive guidance on how units plan, prepare, and execute tactical level air assault operations within offense, defense, stability, and civil support operations.

This manual applies to the Active Army, the Army National Guard/Army National Guard of the United States, and the U.S. Army Reserves unless otherwise stated.

The proponent for this publication is the U.S. Army Training and Doctrine Command. The preparing agency is the U.S. Army Maneuver Center of Excellence (MCoE). You may send comments and recommendations by any means—U.S. mail, e-mail, fax, or telephone—using or following the format of DA Form 2028, *Recommended Changes to Publications and Blank Forms*.

E-mail: BENN.CATD.DOCTRINE@CONUS.ARMY.MIL
Phone: COM 706-545-7114 or DSN 835-7114
Fax: COM 706-545-8511 or DSN 835-8511
U.S. Mail: Commanding General, MCoE
ATTN: ATZB-TDD
Fort Benning, GA 31905-5410

Unless otherwise stated in this publication, masculine nouns and pronouns refer to both men and women.

Summary of Changes

Overall	• Incorporated changes and terms based on FM 3-0. • Replaced references to battlefield operating systems with warfighting functions. • Reduced redundancy whenever possible by referring to other doctrinal publications. • Removed discussions not directly related to the planning, preparation, and execution of air assault operations.		
Ch 1	Additions include— • Operational environment. • Mission command as preferred method of battle command. • Technique for positioning key leadership. Deletions include— • Tenets and combat imperatives of Air Land Battle doctrine. • Organization considerations based on outdated organizational structures. Updates include— • Definitions of air assault and air movement. • Air assault task force organization. • Air assault capabilities, limitations, and vulnerabilities. • Definition of command and control. • Command and control system. ▪ Command post organization. ▪ Key personnel. • Communications equipment and technology. • AC2 integration.	**Ch 5**	• Added Aviation Mission Planning System. • Updated air movement plan development, to include— ▪ Air routes. ▪ Flight designation and dissemination ▪ Airspace coordinating measures. ▪ En route formations. ▪ Terrain flight modes. ▪ Suppression of enemy air defenses. ▪ Air assault security. ▪ Air movement table.
		Ch 6	Updates include— • Loading plan: ▪ Pickup zone selection. ▪ Pickup zone organization and control. ▪ Coordination with supporting aviation unit. ▪ Preparation of air loading tables. ▪ Pickup zone diagram. ▪ Bump plan. • Staging plan: ▪ Preparation for loading. ▪ Movement to pickup zone. ▪ Chalk check-in and inspection. ▪ Load staging.
Ch 2	Additions include— • Roles and responsibilities of air assault task force higher headquarters, brigade combat team, and supporting aviation units in the planning process. • Planning methodology. • Shaping operations. • Execution checks. Deletions include— • Combat preparations, which are incorporated in other areas of the manual. • Operations security and countermeasures. Updates include— • Reverse planning sequence. • Air assault planning process.	**Ch 7**	Updates include— • Attack reconnaissance battalion and squadron organizations. • Fires planning considerations. • Medical evacuation: ▪ Planning considerations. ▪ Execution. ▪ Casualty backhaul. ▪ Landing zone procedures. • Sustainment operations: ▪ General concept of operations. ▪ Preparation. ▪ Air assault task force sustainment operations. ▪ FARP procedures. • Army helicopter characteristics and planning considerations. Deletions include— • Air defense artillery and naval gunfire. • Air Force fixed-wing and engineer systems and capabilities. Additions include— • Ground reconnaissance support. • Pathfinder support.
Ch 3	Additions include— • Commander's intent. • Battlefield organization. • Air-ground integration: ▪ Close combat attack. ▪ Target marking. ▪ Target handover. ▪ Battle damage assessment. ▪ Call for fire. ▪ Clearance of fire.		
Ch 4	• Added landing zone updates, hot landing zone procedures, and exiting the aircraft and landing zone. • Removed combat operations. • Updated landing zone selection.		

This page intentionally left blank.

Chapter 1

Introduction

An air assault is a vertical envelopment conducted to gain a positional advantage, to envelop or to turn enemy forces that may or may not be in a position to oppose the operation. Ideally, the commander seeks to surprise the enemy and achieve an unopposed landing when conducting a vertical envelopment. However, the assault force must prepare for the presence of opposition. At the tactical level, vertical envelopments focus on seizing terrain, destroying specific enemy forces, and interdicting enemy withdrawal routes.

SECTION I – AIR ASSAULTS AND AIR MOVEMENTS

1-1.   An air assault is not synonymous with an air movement. They are separate and distinct missions. Air assaults are not merely movements of Soldiers, weapons, and equipment by Army aviation units and should not be considered as such.

1-2.   An air assault operation is an operation in which assault forces, using the mobility of rotary-wing assets and the total integration of available firepower, maneuver under the control of a ground or air maneuver commander to engage enemy forces or to seize and hold key terrain (JP 3-18). They are precisely planned and vigorously executed combat operations. They allow friendly forces to strike over extended distances and terrain barriers to attack the enemy when and where he is most vulnerable. Commanders and leaders must develop an insight into the principles governing their organization and employment to take advantage of the opportunities offered by air assaults.

1-3.   Army air movements are operations involving the use of utility and cargo rotary-wing aircraft and Army operational support fixed-wing assets for other than air assaults (FM 3-90). Air movements are conducted to move Soldiers and equipment; emplace systems; and transport ammunition, fuel, and other high-value supplies. The same general considerations that apply to air assaults also apply to air movements.

SECTION II – OPERATIONAL ENVIRONMENT

1-4.   Operational environments (OEs) are a composite of the conditions, circumstances, and influences that affect the employment of capabilities and bear on the decisions of the commander (JP 3-0). While they include all enemy, adversary, friendly, and neutral systems across the spectrum of conflict, they also include an understanding of the physical environment, the state of governance, technology, local resources, and the culture of the local population (FM 3-0). The OE in which U.S. units conduct operations is dynamic and complex. Factors that affect the OE include—

- Globalization.
- Technology.
- Demographic changes.
- Urbanization.
- Resource demand.
- Climate change and natural disasters.
- Proliferation of weapons of mass destruction and effects.
- Failed or failing states.

1-5.   States, nations, transnational actors, and nonstate entities will continue to challenge and redefine the global distribution of power, the concept of sovereignty, and the nature of warfare. Threats are nation states, organizations, people, groups, conditions, or natural phenomena able to damage or destroy life, vital resources, or institutions. Preparing for and managing these threats requires employing all instruments of national power, including diplomatic, informational, military, and economic. Threats may be described through a range of four major categories or challenges: traditional, irregular, catastrophic, and disruptive. While helpful in describing the threats the Army is likely to face, these categories do not define the nature of the adversary. In fact, adversaries may use any and all of these challenges in combination to achieve the desired effect against the United States (FM 3-0).

1-6.   Future conflicts are much more likely to be fought among the people instead of around the people. This fundamentally alters the manner in which Soldiers can apply force to achieve success in a conflict. Enemies seek populations within which to hide as protection against the proven attack and detection means of U.S. forces, in preparation for attacks against communities, as refuge from U.S. strikes against their bases, and to draw resources. War remains a battle of wills; it's a contest for dominance over people. The essential struggle of the future conflict will take place in areas in which people are concentrated and will require U.S. security dominance to extend across the population (FM 3-0).

OPERATIONAL VARIABLES

1-7.   When assigning a mission to a subordinate unit, the higher headquarters provides that unit an analysis of the OE, which includes operational variables. The operational variables are factors like political, military, economic, social, information, infrastructure, physical environment, and time that help characterize or describe the aspects of the OE. The subordinate commander and staff refine the information about the operational variables that it receives from its higher headquarters. The commander and staff focus on those aspects that provide relevant information for their use. (See FM 3-0 for details.)

MISSION VARIABLES

1-8.   Army leaders use the mission variables to synthesize operational variables and tactical-level information with local knowledge about conditions relevant to their mission. The mission variables are mission, enemy, terrain and weather, troops and support available, time available, and civil considerations (METT-TC). These are the categories of relevant information used for mission analysis. By incorporating the operational variables into mission analysis, subordinates, commanders, and their staffs increase their understanding of the human aspects of the situation that a mission analysis might otherwise overlook, such as language, culture, history, education, and beliefs. (See FM 3-0 for details.)

SECTION III – ORGANIZATION

1-9.   No existing units below division level are capable of independently conducting air assaults. The battalion is the lowest level organization staffed with sufficient personnel to plan, coordinate, and control an air assault. When company-sized operations are conducted, the predominance of planning occurs at battalion or higher level. Brigade combat teams do not have the organic aviation units to ensure successful air assault mission accomplishment. Task organizing or mission-specific tailoring of forces is the norm for air assaults.

AIR ASSAULT TASK FORCE

1-10. Air assaults are accomplished by forming and employing an air assault task force. The AATF is a temporary group of integrated forces tailored to a specific mission under the command of a single headquarters. It may include some or all elements of the BCT. The ground or air maneuver commander, designated as the air assault task force commander (AATFC), commands the AATF.

1-11. Brigade combat teams and aviation elements from combat aviation brigades are ideally suited to form powerful and flexible AATFs that can project combat power throughout an area of operations (AO) within full spectrum operations with little regard for terrain barriers. The unique versatility and strength of an AATF is achieved by combining the speed, agility, and firepower of rotary-wing aircraft with those of the maneuver forces in the BCTs.

BRIGADE COMBAT TEAMS

1-12. All three types of BCTs—heavy, Stryker, and Infantry—have the capability to plan, prepare, and execute air assault operations when the situation dictates. All BCTs are organized with maneuver, fires, reconnaissance, sustainment, military intelligence, military police, signal, and engineer capabilities. Higher headquarter commanders augment BCTs for a specific mission with capabilities not organic to the BCT structure. (See FM 3-90.6 for details on BCT organization and capabilities.)

1-13. Although heavy brigade combat teams (HBCTs) and Stryker brigade combat teams (SBCTs) may not conduct air assaults as frequently as IBCTs, such operations conducted on a limited scale may be the decisive maneuver in an HBCT or SBCT operation. For this reason, all BCTs should be proficient in conducting air assaults. Examples of air assault operations conducted by HBCTs and SBCTs include seizure and retention of river-crossing sites, deliberate breaches, and seizure of key terrain. Understanding the detailed planning and preparation that goes into an air assault enables the HBCT or SBCT to—

- Exploit the mobility and speed of task-organized or supporting helicopters to secure a key objective in the offense.
- Reinforce a threatened unit in the defense.
- Place combat power at a decisive point in an AO.

1-14. Due to the abundance and unrestricted use of all forms of improvised explosive devices in the OE, it is not uncommon for combined arms battalions, engineer companies, artillery batteries, and reconnaissance troops to conduct air assault operations alongside or separate from their Infantry counterparts. Ground tactical movement subjects the entire organization to the threat of improvised explosive devices as soon as the vehicles leave their assembly areas or forward operating bases.

COMBAT AVIATION BRIGADES

1-15. Most of the Army's aviation combat power resides in CABs, which can be task organized based on the mission (Figure 1-1, Figure 1-2, and Figure 1-3). Combat aviation brigades are organized to support divisions, BCTs, and support brigades. They include various types of organizations with manned and unmanned systems and specialize in providing combat capabilities to multiple BCTs. (See FM 3-04.111 for details.)

1-16. In a BCT-sized air assault, the CAB typically task organizes based on the mission variables to form an aviation task force. Additional aviation companies, platoons, or sections may be task organized to include attack reconnaissance (manned and unmanned), airborne command and control (C2), communications relay, air medical evacuation, and air traffic services. In BCT-sized air assaults, reinforcement with additional aviation is a common way to mass combat power and accelerate force buildup. Other combined arms forces, to include Infantry, field artillery, engineer, or sustainment units, may be part of the CAB task organization for specific missions.

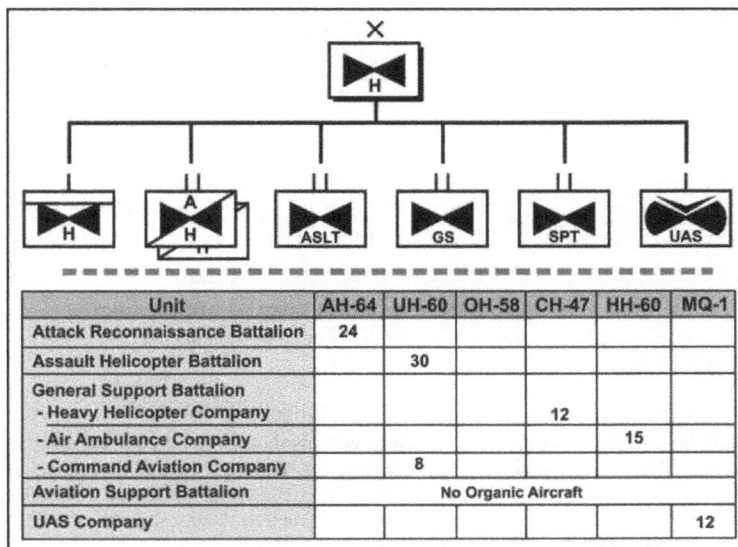

Unit	AH-64	UH-60	OH-58	CH-47	HH-60	MQ-1
Attack Reconnaissance Battalion	24					
Assault Helicopter Battalion		30				
General Support Battalion – Heavy Helicopter Company				12		
– Air Ambulance Company					15	
– Command Aviation Company		8				
Aviation Support Battalion	No Organic Aircraft					
UAS Company						12

Figure 1-1. Heavy combat aviation brigade organization

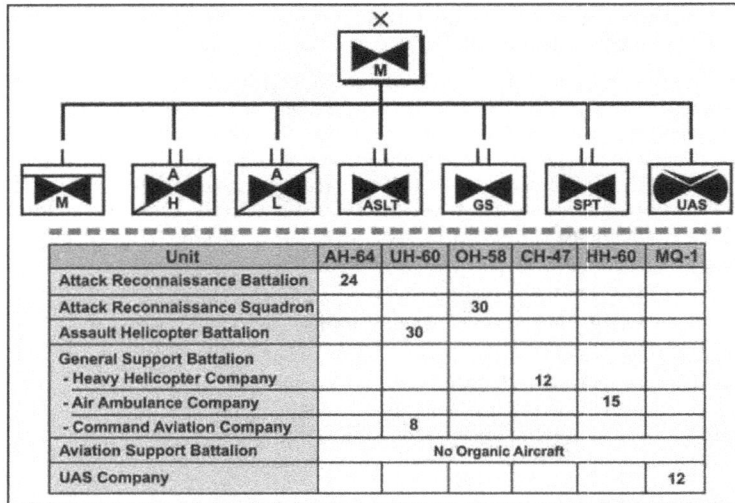

Figure 1-2. Medium combat aviation brigade organization

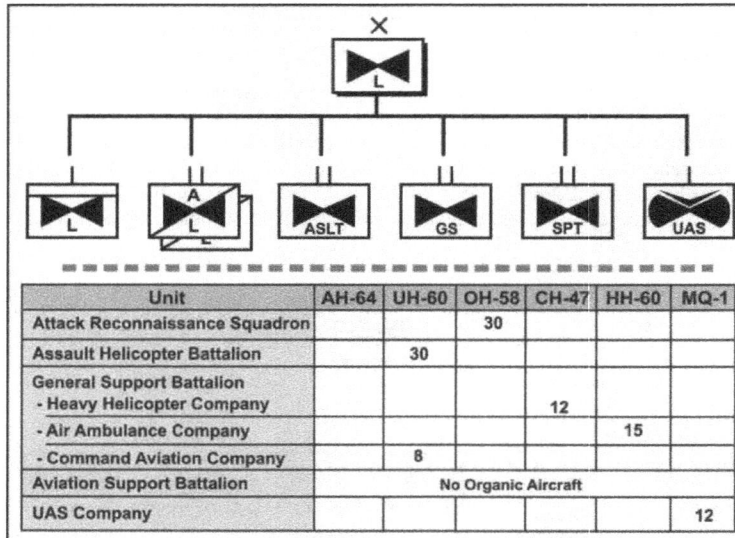

Figure 1-3. Light combat aviation brigade organization

CONSIDERATIONS

1-17. When forming an air assault task force, consider the following factors:

- **Early formation of the AATF.** This force is formed early in the planning stage by a headquarters that can allocate dedicated aviation resources. The directing or establishing headquarters allocates units and defines authority and responsibility by designating command and support relationships. Predesignated and well-understood command and support relationships ensure the AATF fights as a cohesive, coordinated, combined arms team.

- **Availability of aviation assets.** The warning order may include the task organization of the AATF which must provide a mission-specific balance of mobility, combat power, and endurance. It is normally organized with sufficient combat power to seize initial objectives and protect landing zones (LZs). The required combat power should be delivered to the objective area consistent with aircraft and pickup zone (PZ) capacities to take advantage of surprise and shock effect.

● **Maintaining unit tactical integrity.** When planning loads, squads are normally loaded intact on the same helicopter, with platoons located in the same serial, to ensure unit integrity upon landing. To perform its mission, an AATF must arrive intact at the LZ. The force must be tailored to provide en route security and protection from the PZ, throughout the entire air route(s), and at the LZ.

● **Sufficient sustainment capability.** The AATF is organized with a sustainment capability to support a rapid tempo until follow-on or linkup forces arrive, or until the mission is completed. Units that support the air assault operation are normally placed in direct support to the AATF to ensure close coordination and continuous, dedicated support throughout an operation. Normally, an AATF exists only until completion of a specified mission. After that, aviation and other elements return to the control of their parent unit(s).

SECTION IV – EMPLOYMENT

1-18. Air assaults are high-risk, high-payoff missions that, when properly planned and vigorously executed, allow commanders to generate combat power and apply the warfighting functions. An air assault can provide the means for the commander to control the tempo of operations in his AO and enable him to rapidly execute full spectrum operations to retain or exploit the initiative.

1-19. An AATF is most effective in environments where limited lines of communications are available to the enemy that also lacks air superiority and effective air defense systems. It should not be employed in roles requiring deliberate operations over an extended period of time, and is best employed in situations that provide a calculated advantage due to surprise, terrain, threat, or mobility. In particular, an AATF is employed in missions that require—

● Massing or shifting combat power quickly.
● Using surprise.
● Using flexibility, mobility, and speed.
● Gaining and maintaining the initiative.

1-20. The following are basic considerations for the planning and execution of air assaults:

● Air assault operations are best conducted at night or during weather conditions that allow aircraft operation but obscure enemy observation to facilitate deception and surprise.
● Fire support (FS) planning must provide for suppressive fires along air routes and in the vicinity of LZs. Priority for fires should be to the suppression of enemy air defenses (SEAD) systems.
● Infantry unit operations are not fundamentally changed by integrating with aviation units. However, tempo and distance are dramatically changed.
● Ground and aerial reconnaissance units should be employed as early as possible to conduct reconnaissance and surveillance activities in order to shape the operational area for successful execution.

CAPABILITIES

1-21. An AATF can extend the battlefield, move, and rapidly concentrate combat power like no other available forces. Specifically, an AATF can—

● Attack enemy positions from any direction.
● Conduct attacks and raids beyond the operational area.
● Conduct exploitation and pursuit operations.
● Overfly and bypass enemy positions, barriers, and obstacles and strike objectives in otherwise inaccessible areas.
● Provide responsive reserves, allowing commanders to commit a larger portion of his force to action.

- React rapidly to tactical opportunities, necessities, and threats in unassigned areas.
- Rapidly place forces at tactically decisive points in the AO.
- Conduct fast-paced operations over extended distances.
- Conduct and support deception with false insertions.
- Rapidly reinforce committed units.
- Rapidly secure and defend key terrain (such as crossing sites, road junctions, and bridges) or key objectives.
- Delay a much larger force without becoming decisively engaged.

LIMITATIONS

1-22. An AATF relies on helicopter support throughout an air assault operation. As such, they may be limited by—

- Adverse weather; extreme heat and cold; and other environmental conditions (such as blowing snow and sand) that limit flight operations, helicopter lifting capability, or altitude and elevation restrictions that affect operational capabilities.
- Reliance on air lines of communications.
- Threat aircraft, air defense, and electronic warfare action.
- Reduced ground mobility once inserted (particularly HBCT and SBCT forces).
- Availability of suitable LZs and PZs due to mountainous, urban, or other complex terrain.
- Availability of air routes (for example, air routes near international borders).
- Availability of chemical, biological, radiological, and nuclear (CBRN) protection and decontamination capability.
- Battlefield obscuration that limits helicopter flight.
- High fuel and ammunition consumption rates.
- Availability of organic fires, sustainment assets, and protection.

VULNERABILITIES

1-23. An AATF uses helicopters to move to and close with the enemy. Initial assault elements should be light and mobile. They are often separated from weapon systems, equipment, and materiel that provide protection and survivability on the battlefield. An AATF is particularly vulnerable to enemy—

- Attack by aircraft and air defense weapon systems during the movement phase.
- Attack by CBRN weapons because of limited CBRN protection and decontamination capability.
- Attack by ground, air, or artillery during the loading and landing phases.
- Air strikes due to limited availability of air defense weapon systems.
- Electronic attack, including jamming of communications and navigation systems, and disrupting aircraft survivability equipment.
- Small-arms fire that presents a large threat to helicopters during the air movement and landing phases.

SECTION V – COMMAND AND CONTROL

1-24. Command and control is the exercise of authority and direction by a properly designated commander over assigned and attached forces in the accomplishment of a mission (FM 1-02).

- **Command** is the authority that the AATFC and subordinate commanders lawfully exercise over subordinates by virtue of rank or assignment.
- **Control** is the regulation of the AATF and the warfighting functions to accomplish the mission in accordance with the commander's intent.

1-25. The AATFC performs C2 functions through a C2 system. An AATF C2 system includes the procedures, facilities, equipment, and personnel who gather information, make plans, communicate changes, and control all ground and air elements in pursuit of the AATF objective. (See FM 6-0 for details.)

1-26. The Army's two key concepts for exercising C2 are battle command and mission command. Mission command is the Army's preferred means of battle command. (See FM 3-0 for details on battle command and the commander's role in the operations process.)

COMMAND AND CONTROL SYSTEM

1-27. The AATF C2 system consists of the key personnel and equipment in the command posts (CPs). The following describes how the AATFC organizes his CPs to conduct an air assault and lists the key personnel in the air assault C2 system.

COMMAND POST ORGANIZATION

1-28. The AATFC executes C2 of the task force through the establishment of two primary CPs—main CP and tactical CP. If the AATFC is also the BCT commander, he has the option to form a command group consisting of the BCT commander and selected staff members who accompany him and help exercise C2 away from a CP.

Main Command Post

1-29. The main CP provides control of operations when the tactical CP is not deployed. When the tactical CP is deployed, the main CP—

- Provides planning for future operations.
- Maintains current enemy and friendly situations.
- Gathers and disseminates intelligence.
- Keeps higher and adjacent organizations informed of the friendly situation and submits recurring reports.
- Acts as liaison to higher and adjacent organizations.
- Coordinates for and advises the commander on the use of enablers for future operations.
- Assists the tactical CP with executing operations as necessary.
- Develops and disseminates orders as necessary.
- Identifies threat electronic warfare capabilities and plans for countermeasures.

Tactical Command Post

1-30. The AATFC employs the tactical CP as an extension of the main CP to help control execution of the air assault for a limited period of time. The AATF tactical CP may be employed into the objective area soon after the initial echelon if the enemy situation permits. The tactical CP assists the commander in controlling current operations by—

- Maintaining the common operational picture and assisting in developing situational understanding.
- Developing combat intelligence of immediate interest to the commander.
- Maneuvering forces.
- Controlling and coordinating fires.
- Coordinating with adjacent units and forward air defense elements.
- Serving as the main CP if the main CP is destroyed or unable to function.

1-31. The tactical CP consists of the AATFC, representatives from the S-2 and S-3 section, fire support officer (FSO), brigade aviation officer (BAO), and air liaison officer (ALO) or whomever the commander designates. The tactical CP deploys in a C2 aircraft piloted by the air mission commander (AMC). This aircraft contains an airspace command and control (AC2) package, which allows the commander to observe and direct the air assault from a forward position if he chooses. The AATFC may also elect to deploy a tactical CP with the maneuver force. This CP is normally led by the AATF S-3 and consists of a mission-tailored portion of the AATF headquarters.

Command Groups

1-32. The BCT headquarters can form two command groups, which are organized based on the mission. Both are equipped to operate separately from the tactical CP or main CP. Command groups give the commander and the deputy commanding officer the mobility and protection to move throughout the AO and to observe and direct BCT operations from forward positions. (See FM 3-90.6 for details.)

1-33. Both command groups require a dedicated security element when departing the main CP. The command group led by the BCT commander consists of whomever he designates. This can include the sergeant major and representatives from the S-2, S-3, and fires sections. The commander positions his command group near the most critical event, usually with or near the main effort.

1-34. The command group led by the deputy commanding officer, if used, may include the assistant operations officer, assistant intelligence officer, and an FSO. The deputy commanding officer usually positions his command group with a shaping effort or at a location designated by the BCT commander. The deputy commanding officer must be able to communicate with the BCT, the battalion commanders, and the CPs.

KEY PERSONNEL

1-35. The most important elements of the C2 system are the personnel who man the CPs and assist the AATFC by exercising control of the air assault from the planning stage through execution.

Air Assault Task Force Commander

1-36. The AATFC is the overall commander of the AATF. He ensures continuity of command throughout the operation. As in any operation, he must position himself where he can best see the battlefield and control the operation. In situations that allow, he is airborne in a C2 helicopter during the air movement stage. At other times, he may fight the battle from a tactical CP.

Ground Tactical Commander

1-37. The ground tactical commander (GTC) is the commander of the largest ground maneuver force inserted during an air assault. He is usually one of the AATFCs subordinate maneuver commanders (such as battalion or company commander). He flies on one of the first serials into the objective area, maintaining communication with the AATFC during the flight.

Air Mission Commander

1-38. The AMC is the aviation unit commander or his designated representative. He receives and executes the AATFCs guidance and directives, and controls all aviation elements. The AMC ensures continuity of command for all supporting aviation units and employs attack helicopters and artillery along the air route, fighting the battle from PZ to LZ while keeping the AATFC informed.

Air Assault Task Force S-3

1-39. The AATF S-3 assists the AATFC in C2. He normally leads the AATF tactical CP when the AATFC is airborne in a C2 helicopter.

Brigade Aviation Officer

1-40. The BAO advises the AATFC on all matters relating to Army aviation and, along with the AATF S-3 air, jointly develops the detailed plans necessary to support the air assault operation. During the execution phase, he should be available to assist the AATFC or S-3 air in coordinating the employment of aviation units.

Air Defense Airspace Management/Brigade Aviation Element

1-41. The air defense airspace management (ADAM)/brigade aviation element (BAE), led by the BAO, is a functional cell residing in the BCT's main CP that helps coordinate and synchronize the aviation plan with the ground commander's scheme of maneuver. The ADAM/BAE focuses on providing employment advice and initial planning for aviation missions, unmanned aircraft systems (UASs), airspace planning and coordination, and synchronization with the ALO and FSO. The ADAM/BAE also coordinates directly with the aviation brigade or the supporting aviation task force for detailed mission planning. The ADAM/BAE section is equipped with the Tactical Airspace Integration System, which provides a digitized, integrated, and automated system to provide AC2 and air traffic services.

Fire Support Officer

1-42. The AATF FSO plans, coordinates, and synchronizes FS for all phases of the air assault. He normally deploys with the AATFC in a C2 helicopter to ensure the fires plan is executed as planned.

Tactical Operations Officer

1-43. The tactical operations officer from the BAE advises the AATF on all tactical matters relating to Army aviation. The tactical operations officer is the subject matter expert on Army aviation; enemy threat weapons and tactics, techniques, and procedures; aircraft survivability equipment; and mission planning. He should be available during all phases of the operation, especially the execution phase.

Aviation Liaison Officer

1-44. Although the ADAM/BAE conducts many of the functions traditionally performed by liaison officers, the aviation liaison officer (AVN LNO) from the supporting aviation brigade remains a critical part of the air assault planning process. The AVN LNO can be the supporting aviation unit S-3, the tactical operations officer, or another aviation subject matter expert designated by the supporting aviation unit commander.

1-45. While the members of the ADAM/BAE work directly for the BCT commander as permanent members of the staff, AVN LNOs represent the supporting aviation task force at a designated maneuver headquarters only for the duration of a specific operation. If colocated with the ADAM/BAE, the liaison officer team normally reports to the BAO as a functioning addition to the ADAM/BAE staff section. Often, the AVN LNO coordinates with the ADAM/BAE and then proceeds to a supported ground maneuver battalion.

Air Liaison Officer

1-46. The ALO is an Air Force officer who leads the tactical air control party colocated at the BCT headquarters and advises the BCT commander and staff on air operations. The ALO leverages the expertise of the BCT tactical air control party with links to the higher headquarters tactical air control party to plan, coordinate, synchronize, and execute air support operations. He also maintains situational awareness of the total air support and air support effects picture. Additional responsibilities of the ALO include—

- Monitoring the execution of the air tasking order.
- Advising the commander and staff about the employment of air assets.
- Receiving, coordinating, planning, prioritizing, and synchronizing immediate close air support requests.
- Providing Air Force input to analyses and plans.

Pickup Zone Control Officer

1-47. A pickup zone control officer (PZCO) is designated for each PZ in an air assault. The PZCO organizes, controls, and coordinates operations in the PZ. Depending on the unit that is conducting the air assault, the PZCO may be a BCT, battalion, or company executive officer; BCT or battalion S-3 air; or sometimes a company first sergeant. The PZCO operates on the combat aviation net (CAN) and is prepared to assist in executing needed changes as necessary.

MISSION COMMAND

1-48. Mission command is the conduct of military operations through decentralized execution based on mission orders (FM 6-0). Mission command consists of four elements.

- Commander's intent.
- Individual initiative.
- Mission orders.
- Resource allocation.

1-49. The AATFCs intent, formalized in the order and understood at the execution level, provides the AATF with the concept of operations, allowing the task force to act promptly as the situation requires. The commander focuses his order on the purpose of tasks and the air assault operation as a whole rather than on the details of how to perform assigned tasks. Orders and plans are as brief and simple as possible. (See FM 6-0 for details on mission command.)

CENTRALIZED PLANNING AND DECENTRALIZED EXECUTION

1-50. Mission command is the preferred method of C2. However, the AATFC may decide that a detailed command is more appropriate. He considers the complexity of the operation, mission variables, and experience level of his subordinate commanders and staffs. In most situations, air assaults are centrally planned and well rehearsed before execution. This ensures that each subordinate leader knows the commander's intent and is able to execute his mission with minimal command intervention.

1-51. Contingencies or alternative courses of actions should be factored into the plan to allow for continuation of the mission in a dynamic environment. Tasks must be planned to occur based on time or the execution of a previous task (or tasks) so that actions occur at the specified time or in the specified sequence. Manned or unmanned aircraft systems may be used for communications relay to help mitigate potentially degraded or lost communications.

1-52. Another factor for the commander to consider when determining C2 responsibility is the location of the key AATF leadership. Key leaders should be positioned into discrete elements and dispersed throughout the lifts with provisions to ensure continuity of command. Figure 1-4 shows an example for positioning key leaders during an air assault.

1-53. While air assault planning is centralized, air assault execution is aggressive and decentralized. Subordinate commanders should be given as much freedom of action as possible (consistent with tactical risk and mission accomplishment considerations) to ensure mission success.

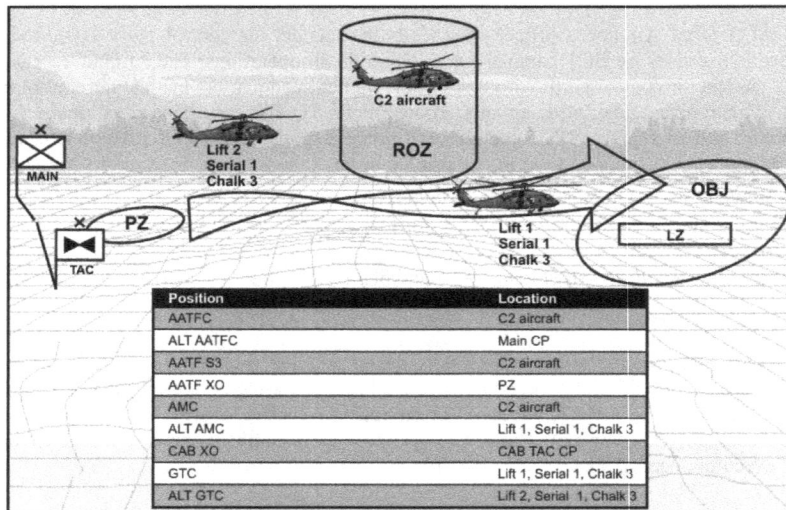

Position	Location
AATFC	C2 aircraft
ALT AATFC	Main CP
AATF S3	C2 aircraft
AATF XO	PZ
AMC	C2 aircraft
ALT AMC	Lift 1, Serial 1, Chalk 3
CAB XO	CAB TAC CP
GTC	Lift 1, Serial 1, Chalk 3
ALT GTC	Lift 2, Serial 1, Chalk 3

Figure 1-4. Example of air assault leadership positioning

SECTION VI – INFORMATION SYSTEMS AND COMMUNICATION

1-54. Information systems enable mission command in an air assault. They enable the AATFC to share the common operating picture with subordinates to guide the exercise of initiative. The common operating picture conveys the commander's perspective and facilitates subordinates' situational understanding.

INFORMATION SYSTEMS

1-55. Information systems that support the AATFCs C2 system include—

ARMY BATTLE COMMAND SYSTEM

1-56. The Army Battle Command System (ABCS) gives the AATF a significant advantage in collecting technical information and distributing information and intelligence rapidly. The ABCS consists of ten core battlefield automated systems plus common services and network management. Each system aids in planning, coordinating, and executing operations by providing access to and the passing of information from a horizontally integrated AATF C2 network. (See FM 3-90.6 for details.)

COMBAT NET RADIOS

1-57. The AATF uses combat net radios (CNRs) primarily for voice C2 transmission and secondarily for data transmission where other data capabilities do not exist. Combat net radios are designed primarily around the single-channel ground and airborne radio system, the single-channel tactical satellite, and the high frequency (HF) radio. (See FM 6-02.53 for details on CNRs and tactical radio systems.)

BLUE FORCE TRACKER

1-58. Air assault task forces equipped with blue force tracker (BFT) are capable of communicating between platforms. The BFT system is an L-band satellite communications tracking system that provides the commander situational awareness of friendly forces and provides the commander with the ability to send and receive text messages. The BFT system is not ABCS-interoperable or compatible with the Enhanced Position Location Reporting System (EPLRS) because it lacks the hardware encrypted secure communications accreditation.

ENHANCED POSITION LOCATION REPORTING SYSTEM

1-59. Brigade combat teams equipped with Force XXI Battle Command, Brigade and Below (FBCB2)-terrestrial use the EPLRS to provide rapid, jam-resistant, secure data transfer between FBCB2 systems. The EPLRS network provides the primary data and imagery communications transmission system. It is employed in the combat platforms of the commander, executive officer, first sergeant, platoon leaders, and platoon sergeants at the company and platoon level.

1-60. The EPLRS is an alternate data communications link (host-to-host) between C2 platforms at the brigade and battalion levels. It is the primary data communications link between battalion C2 platforms and company and platoon combat platforms. The EPLRS can be employed in wireless network extension platforms and can be configured to provide wireless network extension capability.

INTEGRATED SYSTEM CONTROL

1-61. The BCT signal officer S-6 and battalion S-6 sections are the air assault staff proponents responsible for planning and coordinating communications support for each phase of the air assault operation. They use integrated system control to provide communications system network management, control, planning, and support to the AATF. Also known as the tactical internet management system, integrated system control provides network initialization, local area network management services, and an automated system to support the CNR-based wide area network. Features of integrated system control include mission plan management, network planning and engineering, battlefield frequency spectrum management, tactical packet network management, and wide area network management.

1-62. As the AATF executes the mission and distances become extended, communications for C2 become less sophisticated. The AATF must make extensive use of airborne or unattended very high frequency (VHF) retransmission, HF capabilities, and ultrahigh frequency (UHF) tactical satellite. Subordinate elements in the AATF may range beyond multichannel capabilities and radio transmissions, and transmissions may be unintelligible due to enemy electronic countermeasures. As a result, subordinate commanders of the AATF may have to make decisions without being in contact with the AATFC.

RADIO NETS

1-63. Frequency monitoring requirements may be organized into a communications card or matrix and distributed to key leaders, CPs, and other key personnel. (See Chapter 3 for an example communication card.) Using a dynamic mix of air-to-air, air-to-ground, and ground-to-ground radio nets provides the necessary responsiveness and flexibility for air assault C2. Table 1-1 depicts the radio nets commonly employed during air assaults and recommended monitoring requirements for each.

- **Air assault task force command net** is a VHF command net dedicated to ground-to-ground coordination during operations. It is normally secure and used by the AATFC to communicate with his subordinate commanders. Given the range of VHF communication limitations in restrictive terrain, consider alternate means of communications such as UHF tactical satellite or HF when planning an air assault.
- **Combat aviation net** is a VHF net dedicated to air-to-ground coordination during operations. All aviation elements and the remainder of the AATF elements monitor this net before and during air movements. The two combat aviation nets typically employed during an air assault are—
    - CAN 1, which provides common communications between the AATFC, AMC, GTC, and the PZCO.
    - CAN 2, which is usually reserved as an anti-jamming net. The PZCO can use this net to provide terminal guidance to individual flight leads when required.
- **Air battle net** is typically a UHF command net dedicated to air-to-air communications between the AMC and all aviation element leaders. All aviation elements monitor this net and receive instructions from the AMC or the AATFC when he is airborne. This net is normally operated on the lift unit's UHF command frequency if a dedicated ABN (ABN) is not specified in the operation order or air mission brief (AMB).
- **Fire support net** is a VHF net operated by the AATF FS coordinator. All aviation elements must have access to this net to facilitate calls for fire during movements, insertions, and extractions. An artillery quick-fire net is normally used when a supporting battery or battalion is dedicated to an air assault. Plan alternate means of communication, such as tactical satellite, multi-use internet relay chat, and BFT or FBCB2, in case of VHF communication failure.
- **Operations and intelligence net** is a secure VHF net controlled by the S-2 section at the main CP. All routine tactical reports and other intelligence reports are sent on this net, freeing the AATFC net for command and combat critical traffic. The main CPs for all elements of the AATF and supporting aviation units monitor the operations and intelligence net.
- **Aviation internal net** is typically a very high frequency net operated by each aviation element leader for internal use. Using very high frequency radios provides each element leader with a dedicated frequency with which to direct and control individual aircraft, teams, or platoons and to communicate with air traffic control authorities.
- **Pickup zone control net** is a VHF net established by the PZCO for communications between ground forces at the PZ. The PZCO may request to use the communication platform from an AC2 UH-60 if it is available. The PZCO uses this net to control the flow of vehicles in and around the PZ. He communicates with the PZ control party on this net. This ensures that chalks are lined up correctly, external loads (sling loads) are ready, the bump plan is activated if necessary, and extraneous vehicles and personnel are kept clear of PZ operations. All lifted units should enter the PZ control net 30 minutes prior to their PZ time. Specific chalks may be required to monitor the net if the aircraft formation in the PZ requires them.

Table 1-1. Standard air assault radio nets and monitoring requirements

	AATF Command Net	CAN 1	CAN 2	ABN	FS/Quick-Fire Net	O&I Net	AVN TF Net	PZ Control Net
AATFC	X	X		X		X		
GTC	X	X			X	X		
AMC	X	X		X	X		X	
FSO		X	X	X				
AVN LNO		X		X			X	
PZCO		X	X					X
Lifted Unit	X	X	X		X	X		X
Legend								

AATF	air assault task force		FS	fire support
AATFC	air assault task force commander		FSO	fire support officer
ABN	air battle net		GTC	ground tactical commander
AVN LNO	aviation liaison officer		O&I	operations and intelligence
CAN	combat aviation net		TF	task force

SECTION VII – AIRSPACE COMMAND AND CONTROL

1-64. Airspace control is a process used to increase operational effectiveness by promoting the safe, efficient, and flexible use of airspace with minimum restraint upon airspace users. It includes coordinating, integrating, and regulating airspace to increase operational effectiveness. Effective airspace control reduces the risk of fratricide, enhances air defense, and permits flexibility (JP 3-52).

1-65. Airspace command and control is the application of airspace control to coordinate airspace users for concurrent employment in assigned missions. Effective AC2 enables all warfighting functions to work efficiently while synchronizing air operations to support the commander's intent. Successful AC2 is dependent on the ability to perform the functions of identification, coordination, integration, and regulation of airspace users (FM 3-52).

1-66. Airspace command and control does not denote ownership of a block of airspace or command over activities within that airspace. Rather, it refers to users of the airspace (FM 3-52). All air missions are subject to the airspace control order (ACO) published by the airspace control authority, which provides direction to deconflict, coordinate, and integrate the use of airspace within the operational area.

1-67. Joint forces also use airspace to conduct air operations, deliver fires, employ air defense measures, and conduct intelligence operations. At times, these missions may be time sensitive and preclude the ability to conduct detailed coordination with the land force. It is imperative that land forces provide their higher headquarters with all airspace control measures in order to provide visibility to other joint users and prevent fratricide.

METHODS

1-68. Methods of airspace control are—

- **Positive control** relies on positive identification, tracking, and direction of aircraft within the airspace control area. It uses electronic means such as radar; sensors; identification, friend or foe systems; selective identification feature capabilities; digital data links; and other elements of the intelligence system and C2 network structures (FM 3-52).
- **Procedural control** relies on a combination of mutually agreed and promulgated orders and procedures. These may include comprehensive air defense identification procedures and rules of engagement, aircraft identification maneuvers, FS coordinating measures, and airspace control measures. Service, joint, and multinational capabilities and requirements determine which method, or which elements of each method, that airspace control plans and systems use (FM 3-52). Procedural control is a common method used by all airspace users (to include indirect fire units) to

deconflict airspace. In Army rotary-wing operations, such as air assaults, procedural control is used more often than positive control.

AIRSPACE COORDINATING MEASURES

1-69. Airspace coordinating measures are measures employed to facilitate the efficient use of airspace to accomplish missions and simultaneously provide safeguards for friendly forces (JP 3-52). (See FM 3-52 for details on joint and Army airspace coordinating measures.)

1-70. Common airspace coordinating measures used during an air assault are—

- **Coordinating altitudes** use altitude to separate users and as the transition between different airspace coordinating entities (JP 3-52). The airspace coordinating entities should be included in the air control plan and promulgated in the ACO. Army echelons incorporate air control plan guidance and integrate the ACO, area air defense plan, special instructions, and air tasking order via operation orders. All airspace users should coordinate with the appropriate airspace coordinating entities when transitioning through or firing through the coordinating altitude.
- **Restricted operations areas** are airspaces of defined dimensions created in response to specific operational situations or requirements within which the operation of one or more airspace users is restricted. They are also known as restricted operations zones (ROZs) (JP 3-52). The AATF may use a restricted operations area or ROZ to procedurally deconflict any area where prior coordination enhances aviation safety.
- **Standard use Army aircraft flight routes** are routes established below the coordinating altitude to facilitate the movement of Army aviation assets. They are normally located in the corps through brigade support areas and do not require approval of the airspace control authority (JP 3-52). They are normally listed on the current ACO. Direction of travel can be dictated as one- or two-way traffic.
- **Air corridors** are restricted air routes of travel specified for use by friendly aircraft and established for the purpose of preventing friendly aircraft from being fired on by friendly forces (JP 3-52). They are used to route aviation combat elements between such areas as forward arming and refueling points, holding areas, and battle positions. Altitudes of an air corridor do not exceed the established coordinating altitude.
- **Axis of advance** is a general route of advance, assigned for the purposes of control, which extends toward the enemy. The axis of advance symbol graphically portrays a commander's intention, such as avoiding built-up areas or known enemy air defense sites. When used for attack aviation operations, it provides the general direction of movement and may be subdivided into routes (FM 3-90).
- **Air control points** are points easily identifiable on the terrain or an electronic navigational aid used to provide necessary control during air movement. Air control points are generally designated at each point where the air route or air corridor makes a definite change in any direction and at any other point deemed necessary for timing or control of the operation (FM 3-52).
- **Communication checkpoints** are points along the air route where serial commanders report to the AMC. Radio transmissions should be used only when necessary. If a report is required, consider using codes to ensure a short transmission.

TECHNIQUES AND PROCEDURES

1-71. Techniques and procedures for airspace control follow.

AIR ROUTE PLANNING

1-72. When developing a course of action, the ground maneuver unit should plan an air axis of advance. This provides the general concept to the aviation planners who further refine it into routes with enough guidance to determine the direction from which the commander wants to approach. The developed axis of advance is not submitted to the higher headquarters AC2 element.

1-73. Upon receipt of the course of action, the aviation unit liaison officer plans the air routes within the air axis of advance. The aviation unit normally plans multiple routes within the axis of advance since the threat air defense disposition may not be clear. The ADAM/BAE should assist in route planning, but the supporting aviation unit is responsible for completing the routes and submitting them to the higher headquarters AC2 element for inclusion on the ACO.

RESTRICTED OPERATIONS ZONE PLANNING

1-74. Any unit with organic UASs is responsible for planning their own ROZs for unmanned aircraft launch and recovery. All elements operating UASs in a BCT submit their request through the ADAM/BAE for deconfliction prior to submitting it to the higher headquarters AC2 element.

1-75. Unmanned aircraft launch and recovery ROZs should typically be 3 kilometers in radius or surface to coordinating altitude, but may be tailored to meet operational requirements. Due to their size, unmanned aircraft launch and recovery ROZs should not be planned near indirect fire units, supporting aviation unit assembly areas, or forward arming and refueling points (FARPs) if possible.

1-76. The supporting CAB submits ROZ locations for C2 and medical evacuation (MEDEVAC) aircraft to the higher headquarters AC2 element. Command and control and MEDEVAC aircraft ROZs should be a minimum of 3 by 3 kilometers in size. The CAB plans both a primary and alternate ROZ for each aircraft. This enables control of the operation as it moves forward and provides a ROZ, if needed, for the higher headquarters mobile command group. Fire support units can utilize ROZs to assist in the deconfliction of airspace between firing locations and target locations.

1-77. Special consideration should be given to any planned employment of an organic UAS near an LZ. If required due to the tactical mission, UASs should be clearly separated by a defined terrain feature from the LZ area, and the approach and exit routes of aircraft.

OBJECTIVE AREA DECONFLICTION

1-78. The three techniques to deconflict airspace between attack reconnaissance aircraft and assault aircraft on the objective are described in the following paragraphs.

Grid Line or Terrain Feature Separation

1-79. This is the most restrictive but easiest technique to execute. It may not allow the attack reconnaissance units to engage targets in the close combat attack (CCA) role during the air assault, but this technique is appropriate when time is limited for rehearsals, or when prior planning is extremely limited or not possible. With this technique, the attack reconnaissance units clear the airspace for inbound assault units by moving to a designated grid line or terrain feature on either side of the objective. This movement and the subsequent maneuver of the attack reconnaissance units in and around the objective area are normally executed in accordance with the instructions in the order. (See Figure 1-5.)

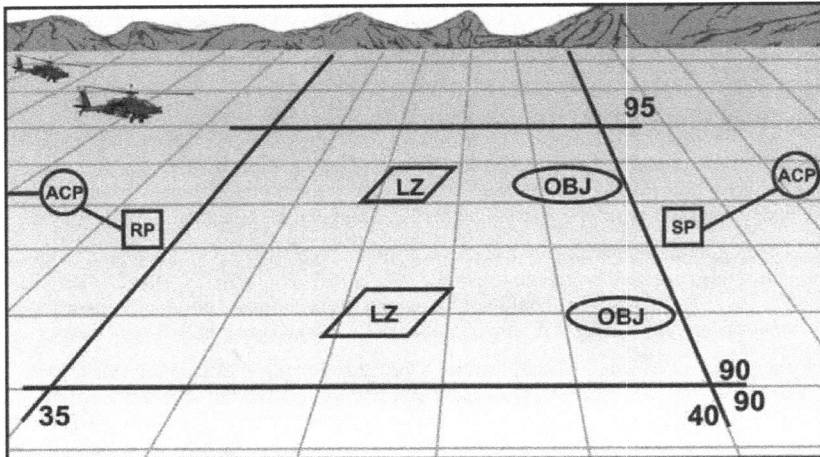

Figure 1-5. Grid line method

Attack-by-Fire Positioning

1-80. Attack-by-fire positioning is the preferred technique of deconfliction, as it allows attack reconnaissance aircraft the greatest flexibility to engage targets during the air assault in support of the GTC. The attack reconnaissance units occupy known attack-by-fire positions in accordance with the published operation order. This method restricts the attack reconnaissance units to the general vicinity of the attack-by-fire positions but not to a specific grid.

1-81. The attack-by-fire positioning technique requires the attack reconnaissance units to ensure they stay clear of the LZ and do not cross the center line of the direction of flight. Using this technique requires the attack reconnaissance aircraft to have increased situational awareness. This technique is best used when all elements have adequate time to rehearse. (See Figure 1-6.)

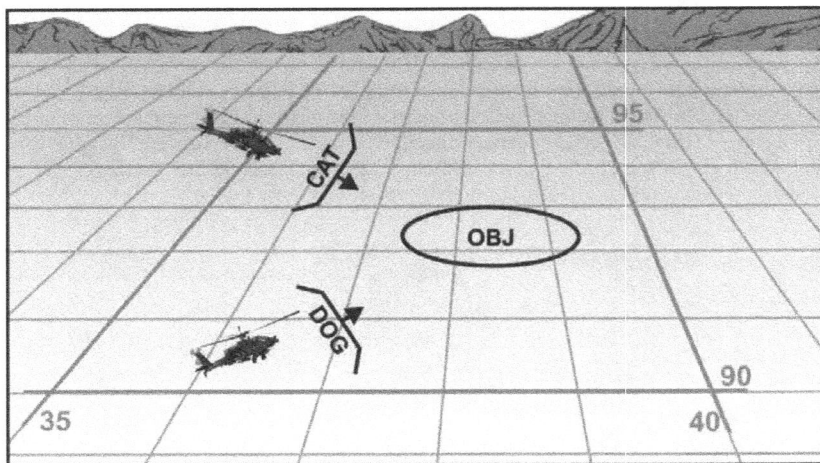

Figure 1-6. Attack-by-fire method

Call Clear

1-82. The call clear technique is used in contingency circumstances when assault or other aircraft (such as MEDEVAC or C2 aircraft) are inbound to the objective area. It is initiated with an inbound call of the assault or other aircraft to the LZ and a response from the attack reconnaissance AMC indicating that all elements of the LZ and the flight path to it from the release point (RP) are clear. Avoid using this method during the main air assault itself due to congestion on the ABN.

Chapter 2

Air Assault Planning

Planning for air assault operations mirrors the military decision-making process (MDMP). It incorporates parallel and collaborative planning actions necessary to provide the additional time and detailed planning required for successful execution of the air assault mission. The standardization of operations between units conducting the air assault significantly enhances the ability of the units to accomplish the mission. Subsequent chapters of this manual discuss each of the air assault planning steps in detail.

SECTION I – REVERSE PLANNING SEQUENCE

2-1. Air assault planning is based on careful analysis of the mission variables and detailed reverse planning. Five basic plans comprise the reverse planning sequence (Figure 2-1):

- Ground tactical plan.
- Landing plan.
- Air movement plan.
- Loading plan.
- Staging plan.

2-2. These plans are not developed independently. The AATF staff and supporting aviation unit coordinate, develop, and refine concurrently to make best use of available time and resources. They develop first the ground tactical plan, which serves as the basis for developing the other plans. Each plan may potentially affect the others. Changes in an aspect of one plan may require adjustments in the other plans. The AATFC must determine if such adjustments entail acceptable risk. If the risk is unacceptable, the concept of operations must change.

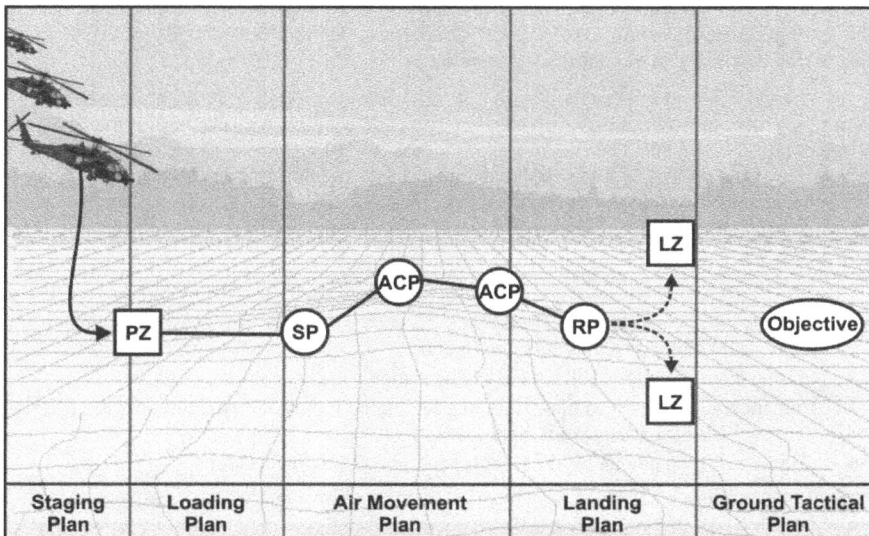

Figure 2-1. Air assault planning stages

SECTION II – ROLES AND RESPONSIBILITIES

2-3.   Air assault planning is as detailed as time permits and should include completion of written orders and plans. Within time constraints, the AATFC carefully evaluates capabilities and limitations of the total force and develops a plan that ensures a high probability of success. The planning time should abide by the "one-third/two-thirds rule" to ensure subordinates have enough time to plan and rehearse.

HIGHER HEADQUARTERS

2-4.   The headquarters above the element forming the AATF directs the formation of the AATF. This headquarters allocates units, defines authority, and assigns responsibility by designating command and support relationships. The staff of this headquarters is responsible for developing the task organization of the AATF and conducting the necessary steps of the MDMP. A division-level commander or his equivalent is the approving authority for the formation of an AATF larger than a company.

BRIGADE COMBAT TEAM

2-5.   The BCT is the core of the air assault and the BCT commander is normally the AATFC for a battalion air assault. The AATFC for a company air assault is normally the battalion commander of the company conducting the assault. The primary role of the AATFC and his staff is to develop the ground tactical plan by providing his staff and the supporting aviation unit staff with key tasks, intent and aviation staff guidance concerning the weight of the attack reconnaissance coverage and the level of acceptable risk for the supporting aviation units.

SUPPORTING AVIATION UNITS

2-6.   Normally, supporting aviation units are under the operational control (OPCON) of the AATFC. Occasionally, an aviation task force may be created to support an AATF. However, the CAB commander typically anticipates the needs of the AATFC and provides the necessary aviation units to support the mission of the AATF. As the supporting unit, the CAB commander directs aviation units within his command or requests augmentation from his higher headquarters to meet the needs of the AATFC.

SECTION III – PLANNING METHODOLOGY

2-7.   The AATF staff conducts continuous coordination under the guidance of the AATF executive officer and S-3 during course of action development. Concurrent planning includes identification of air assault hazards and the development of controls to mitigate risk.

2-8.   The ADAM/BAE and the supporting AVN LNO from the CAB serve as the link between the CAB staff and the AATF staff and are critical to the air assault planning process during mission analysis and course of action development. The ADAM/BAE and the AVN LNO serve as the subject matter experts on aviation operations to the AATF and supported unit staffs during this process. This enables the AATFC and GTC to concentrate on refining the ground tactical plan and follow-on missions. The ADAM/BAE must anticipate requirements of the supported unit(s) and disseminate these requirements as soon as possible to the AVN LNO.

2-9.   The AATF, supported unit(s) staffs, and supporting aviation unit staff should receive and share—

- Landing zone confirmations by imagery, aircraft videos, LZ sketches, reconnaissance products, patrols, and higher headquarters intelligence.
- Composition of assault, follow-on, and operational area echelons by unit.
- Nomenclature of every vehicle and sling load to be flown and maximum expected weight and air item availability for heavy and light loads.
- Confirmed troop counts by serial for assault and follow-on echelons.

2-10. The collaboration between the AATF, supported unit staff, and supporting aviation unit staff results in the Air Assault Appendix to the operation order and may include—

- Tentative lift and serial composition (draft air movement table).

- List of suitable PZs and LZs.
- Tentative air routes.
- LZ imagery (if available).
- Any deviations from standard planning factors.
- An execution checklist.

DELIBERATE PLANNING

2-11. Air assaults are deliberately planned due to the complex nature and requirement to provide the commander detailed intelligence concerning the enemy situation. The air assault planning process mirrors the steps in the MDMP and incorporates parallel actions necessary to provide the additional time and detailed planning required for successful mission execution. Figure 2-2 provides a comparison of the MDMP and the air assault planning process when maximum time is available for planning.

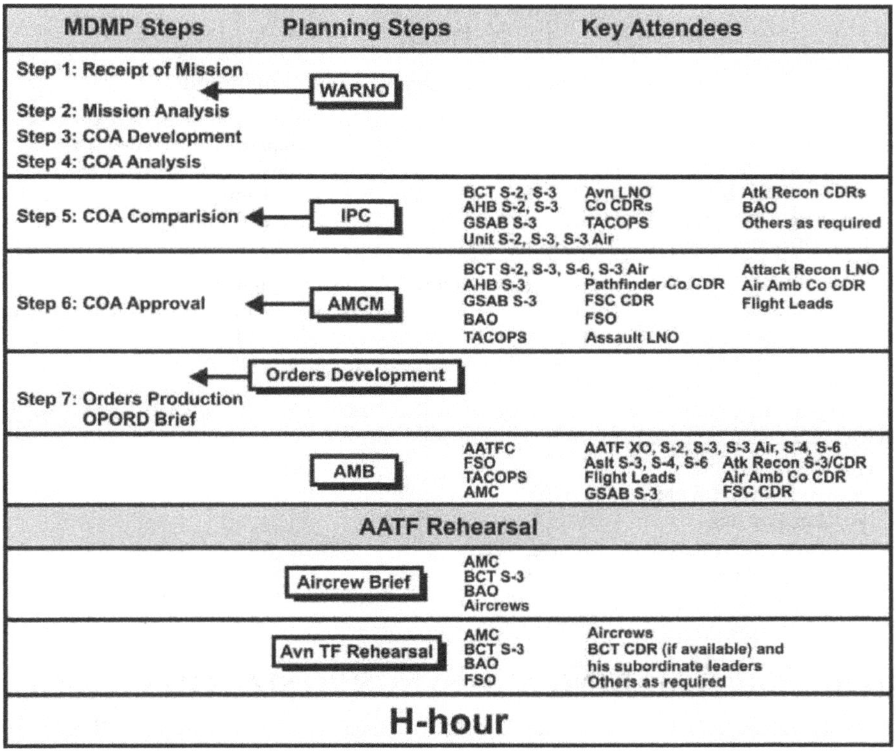

Figure 2-2. Military decision-making process and air assault planning process

TIME-CONSTRAINED PLANNING

2-12. Due to the dynamic nature of full spectrum operations, units are often required to execute air assaults within short time constraints, sometimes a few hours from the time of receiving the operation order. Based on the time available, the AATF executive officer adjusts the timeline as required. It is critical for the executive officer to consider the ability of the supporting aviation unit to accomplish its tasks with its crew endurance program. (See Figure 2-3.)

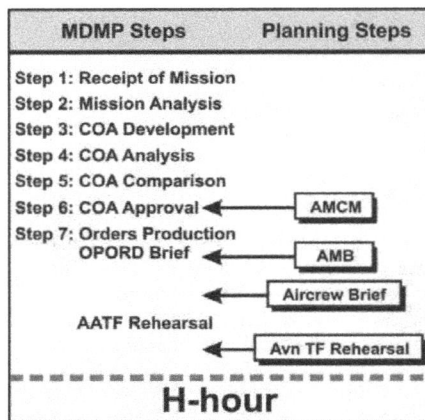

Figure 2-3. Time-constrained air assault planning

2-13. Successful execution of an air assault in a time-constrained environment requires parallel and collaborative planning by all units and staffs that are part of or supporting the AATF. Parallel planning begins as soon as the mission is received, with the supporting CAB providing liaison officers or coordinates through the ADAM/BAE to the AATF if they are not already present. Through continual coordination with the supporting CAB, the ADAM/BAE advises the AATF S-3 on any limitations of aircraft or crew availability affecting course of action development.

2-14. Once the AATFC has provided a directed course of action or approved a course of action, the BAO immediately begins the air mission coordination meeting (AMCM). In order to save time by reducing the number of meetings, specific portions of the AMB are included in the AATF operation order brief in lieu of doing a separate AMB. With the exception of the combined operation order and AMB, mission coordination and planning may be completed by phone, e-mail, video teleconferencing, or other C2 systems. Backbriefs, aircrew briefs, and rehearsals are still conducted as described earlier. The specific portions of the AMB included in the operation order brief are—

- Staging plan.
- Air movement plan.
- Landing plan.
- Attack reconnaissance coverage.
- LZ condition criteria.
- Weather decision.
- Risk assessment.

RAPID DECISION-MAKING AND SYNCHRONIZATION PROCESS

2-15. Typically, the AATFC executes air assaults in response to time-sensitive intelligence or rapidly changing battlefield conditions. If time is extremely limited, the AATFC may choose to rely on his intuition and direct the staff to use the rapid decision-making and synchronization process (RDSP). While the MDMP seeks the optimal solution, the RDSP seeks a timely and effective solution within the commander's intent, mission, concept of operations, and acceptable level of tactical risk. Using the RDSP lets the staffs avoid the time-consuming requirements of developing and comparing multiple courses of action. (See FM 5-0 for details on the RDSP.)

2-16. Due to a shortage of time, the primary method of coordination for the AMCM and the AMB may be via video teleconference or conference call. However, a face-to-face meeting addressing the contents of the AMB should be conducted prior to mission execution. This meeting may be conducted on the PZ with aircraft shutdown. At a minimum, the flight lead, AMC, chalk leaders, S-2, and the GTC should be present. Rehearsals conducted in this situation should be combined AATF and aviation unit events.

ALLOWABLE CARGO LOAD PLANNING CONSIDERATIONS

2-17. To efficiently load an AATF aboard helicopters, commanders and staffs must know the exact composition of the AATF, the essential characteristics of the types of helicopters to be used for the operation, and the methods of computing aircraft requirements.

2-18. Maximum ACL is affected by altitude and temperature and will differ widely according to topography and climatic conditions common to specific zones or areas of military operations. ACLs will further vary based on the location of, approaches to, and exits from LZs; pilot proficiency; aviation unit SOP; type of engine in the aircraft; and age of both aircraft and aircraft engine. Therefore, two identical aircraft, of the same model and type, may not be able to pick up and carry identical loads.

SECTION IV – PLANNING PROCESS

2-19. Throughout the operations process, the AATFCs and staffs synchronize the warfighting functions to accomplish missions. Commanders and staffs use several integrating processes to do this. Where synchronization is the arrangement of action in time, space, and purpose, integration is the combination of actions into a unified whole.

2-20. Integrating processes combine efforts of the AATFC and staff to synchronize specific functions throughout the operations process. The integrating process includes—
- Intelligence preparation of the battlefield. (See FM 2-01.3.)
- Targeting. (See FM 6-20.10.)
- Intelligence, surveillance, and reconnaissance synchronization. (See TC 2-01.)
- Composite risk management. (See FM 5-19.)
- Knowledge management. (See FM 6-01.1.)

2-21. The AATFC and staff also ensure several activities are continuously planned for and coordinated. The following continuing activities require particular concern of the commander and staff throughout the operations process:
- Intelligence, surveillance, and reconnaissance. (See TC 2-01.)
- Security operations. (See FM 3-90.)
- Protection. (See FM 3-37.)
- Liaison and coordination. (See FM 6-0.)
- Terrain management. (See FM 3-90.)
- Information management. (See FM 6-0.)
- AC2. (See FM 3-52.)

2-22. The MDMP integrates activities of the commander, staff, subordinate commanders, and other military and civilian partners when developing an air assault operation order. The AATF staff fosters a shared understanding of the situation as it develops a synchronized plan or order to accomplish a mission. The MDMP not only integrates the actions of the commander, staff, subordinate commanders, and others but also integrates several processes, such as intelligence preparation of the battlefield; intelligence, surveillance, and reconnaissance synchronization and integration targeting; and AC2.

WARNING ORDER

2-23. Air assault planning begins when the designated AATF receives a warning order from higher headquarters for the upcoming air assault mission. The warning order specifies the AATFC and task organization. This allows the aviation commander to dispatch a liaison officer to the AATF headquarters early in the planning phase. Other warning orders and fragmentary orders should follow as the AATF staff and commander work through the reverse planning sequence.

2-24. The following information is sent out with the warning order to provide units in the AATF the information needed for planning:
- Ground tactical commander's scheme of maneuver.
- Estimate of the size of the force to be air assaulted.

- Likely PZs and LZs.
- Air assault task force commander's intent on the number of lifts and general timeline.
- Initial estimate on requirements for attack reconnaissance aircraft.

INITIAL PLANNING CONFERENCE

2-25. The initial planning conference (IPC) is the first meeting between the AATF staff and supporting aviation unit. The AMC, liaison officer, assault helicopter battalion S-2 and S-3, flight leads, and select aviation brigade staff personnel should represent the aviation unit. This initial meeting allows the supporting aviation unit planners to address any impacts that environmental factors (climate and weather, terrain, and altitude) may have on the performance capabilities of the aircraft and subsequent mission accomplishment with the AATF planners, as early as possible in the planning process. The IPC is generally held at the air assault task force headquarters.

2-26. The AATF staff should have hastily war-gamed the concept for the ground tactical plan before the IPC in order for assembled planners to discuss and determine LZs, routes, and PZs. If more planning time exists, units may conduct a subsequent AMCM (similar to the IPC), but this occurs after the ground tactical plan and other mission details are finalized.

2-27. Following the IPC, the ground and aviation staffs should understand the distance and general time involved for each lift. The staffs should know which forces are planned to be in the first lift and in each serial of the first lift, and which first-lift serials are going to which LZs and by what route. Subsequent lifts and follow-on echelon lifts, while discussed at the IPC, can be planned in detail at a later AMCM if time permits.

AIR MISSION COORDINATION MEETING

2-28. The AMCM is a meeting between the AATF and supporting aviation units. It is an S-3-level meeting that follows the development of the ground tactical plan. The AMCM is run by the BAE and chaired by the AATF S-3. The AMCM is scheduled to allow sufficient time for maneuver units to decide on a specific course of action based on the warning order and the standard planning factors.

2-29. The AATFC should approve the maneuver course of action prior to the AMCM. At the AMCM, unit S-3s brief the concept of their ground tactical plans. Specifically, unit S-3s show the composition of combat power, by echelon, required at each LZ. It is imperative that the subordinate unit S-3s attend this meeting with an 80 to 90 percent solution on their requirements.

2-30. The meeting is not complete until the assault helicopter battalion liaison officers know which loads go to which LZ and in what sequence. Attack reconnaissance battalion liaison officers must know the air routes to be used, and all must understand the LZs and agree on a tentative air movement table (with the start and end times of the first and last serial on the LZ). The BAE is the central figure in coordinating this information.

2-31. The AATF S-3, executive officer, commander, or deputy commander must approve changes after the AMCM. It is critical that the supported unit and the air assault planners come to the AMCM with the information needed for an effective meeting. Table 2-1 lists an example AMCM agenda which helps guide the AMCM. The end result of the AMCM is a finalized air movement plan, landing plan, air routes, PZs, and LZs.

Table 2-1. Example air mission coordination meeting agenda

Roll call	BAO/S-3 Air
Intelligence update	AATF S-2
Weather	AATF S-2
Ground tactical plan	AATF S-3
Air movement plan	AHB LNO
Attack reconnaissance aviation concept	ARB LNO
Fires	AATF FSO
C2 plan	AATF S-6
Medical and casualty evacuation plan	AATF Forward Support MEDEVAC Team LNO/S-1/S-4
Refueling plan	AHB LNO
Load plan	BAO/S-3 Air
Review decisions	AATF S-3
S-3 closing comments	AATF S-3
Note. If reconnaissance or pathfinder insertions are planned, also cover emergency extraction plan/trigger, alternate communications plan, rehearsals, communications check, and final coordination. For artillery raids, include laager time/location and trigger for extraction.	

AIR MISSION BRIEF

2-32. Air mission brief refers to the written product and the briefing itself. (See FM 3-04.113 for details on the AMB format.) The AMB is a coordinated staff effort during which the AATFC approves the air assault plan. The AMB is an adjunct to the AATF operation order and is typically published as an appendix to the operations annex. (See FM 5-0 for details on orders preparations.)

2-33. The AMB highlights air assault requirements to the AATF, aviation, and ground units. It should not be a working meeting. It is essentially a backbrief to the AATFC and, equally important, to the key subordinate aviation and ground unit leaders who will execute the mission. The CAB or supporting aviation unit staff plays a vital role in the AMB process.

2-34. The AMB should focus on assault and attack concepts, sequence of events, and the reasoning for the mission's sequence. The slightest change in serial separation, LZs, or other elements of the mission can significantly affect the rest of the plan. The AATFC must approve any changes to the air assault mission after the AMB. It is very difficult to resynchronize the different warfighting functions in the short time that remains between the AMB and mission execution.

Note. In the following figures, unit information is highlighted so that the reader can follow how that information is recorded in each document that supports the AMB.

AIR MOVEMENT TABLE

2-35. The air movement table (Figure 2-4) regulates the sequence of flight operations from PZ to LZ.
- **Line #.** Quick reference with brevity. Numbered sequentially.
- **Aviation unit.** Aviation unit conducting that event. Depicted as units designation over call sign to save space.
- **Lifted unit.** Unit being lifted or air assaulted. If more than one unit is in the load, use unit with most assets in the load. Depicted as units designation over call sign to save space.
- **Lift.** Group of serials that make one complete turn out to and back from the AO. Numbered sequentially.
- **Serial.** Group of the same type of aircraft. The capacity of the smallest LZ determines the number of aircraft in each serial.
- **Chalk.** Each aircraft equals one load. Number UH-60 and CH-47 chalk separately.

- **PZ.** Name of the PZ where chalks pick up the loads.
- **PZ arrival and load time.** Time the troops get on the aircraft or when the aircraft starts to hookup the load.
- **Takeoff time.** Time the aircraft lifts off the PZ.
- **SP time.** Time the aircraft hit the start point (BAE-determined point usually 3 to 5 kilometers from the PZ).
- **RP time.** Time the aircraft hit the release point (BAE-determined point usually 3 to 5 kilometers from the LZ).
- **LZ.** Landing zone name and location determined by the lifted unit's ground tactical plan.
- **LZ time.** Time the serial lands in the landing zone.
- **LZ degree.** Compass heading at which the serial will be landing. Should be converted to and shown in magnetic heading for the aircraft.
- **LZ formation.** Landing formation, normally the trail formation.
- **Routes.** Primary ingress and egress routes for the mission.
- **Load.** Personnel and sling load configuration. Refer to the tadpole diagram to save space on this page.
- **Remarks.** Additional remarks (such as scheduled delays, refuel, or any other uncommon serial characteristics).

Air movement table

Line #	Avn Unit	Lifted Unit	Lift #	Serial	Chalk	PZ	PZ Arr/Load Time	T/O Time	SP Time	RP Time	LZ	LZ Time	LZ Hdg	LZ Form	Routes Ingress	Routes Egress	Load PAX	Load Sling	Remarks
1	4-379	SCT/1-603 IN				As per coord	As per coord				Raven	H-36+00:00	As per PIC	As per PIC	As per PIC	As per PIC	16		False into Lark. To recon Robin
2	4-354	SCT/2-603 IN				As per coord	As per coord				Oriole	H-35+59:00	As per PIC	As per PIC	As per PIC	As per PIC	16		False into Bluejay To recon Sparrow
3	3-354	2/C/6-4 CAV (-)				As per coord	As per coord				Pelican	H-35+58:00	As per PIC	As per PIC	As per PIC	As per PIC	20		False into Emu To recon Crow
4	3-354	2/C/6-4 CAV (-)				As per coord	As per coord				Dove	H-35+57:00	As per PIC	As per PIC	As per PIC	As per PIC	8		False into Cardinal To recon Eagle
5	2-344	A/6-4 CAV	1	1	1-5	Oak	H-3+00:00	H-48:40	H-44:21	H-02:22	Crow	H-Hour	134	TRL	Gold (Crow)	Silver (Crow)	6 per a/c (30)	10x M1151	Refuel FARP EXXON
6	2-344	A/6-4 CAV	1	2	6-9	Oak	H-3+00:00	H-47:40	H-43:21	H-01:22	Crow	H+01:00	134	TRL	Gold (Crow)	Silver (Crow)	6 per a/c (24)	8x M1151	Refuel FARP EXXON
7	2-344	C/6-4 CAV (-)	1	3	10-12	Oak	H-3+00:00	H-46:40	H-42:21	H-00:22	Crow	H+02:00	134	TRL	Gold (Crow)	Silver (Crow)	6 per a/c + 40 (52)	4x M998	Refuel FARP EXXON
8	4-379	A/1-603 IN	2	1	1-5	Maple	H-2+00:00	H-44:40	H-40:21	H+01:38	Robin	H+02:58	112	TRL	Gold (Robin)	Silver (Robin)	5x16 (80)		
9	4-379	A/1-603 IN, HHC/1-603 IN	2	2	6-9	Maple	H-2+00:00	H-43:40	H-39:21	H+02:38	Robin	H+03:58	112	TRL	Gold (Robin)	Silver (Robin)	4x16 (64)		Chalk 9 is the BN CP
10	4-379	B/1-603 IN	2	3	10-14	Maple	H-2+00:00	H-42:40	H-38:21	H+03:38	Robin	H+04:58	112	TRL	Gold (Robin)	Silver (Robin)	5x16 (80)		
11	4-379	B/1-603 IN, 1/E/603 EN	2	4	15-18	Maple	H-2+00:00	H-41:40	H-37:21	H+04:38	Robin	H+05:58	112	TRL	Gold (Robin)	Silver (Robin)	4x16 (64)		Chalk 18 is 1/E/603 EN
12	3-354	D/1-603 IN	3	1	13-16	Oak	H-3+00:00	H-40:40	H-36:21	H+05:38	Robin	H+06:58	112	TRL	Gold (Robin)	Silver (Robin)	8 per a/c (32)	8x M1151	Refuel FARP EXXON

Figure 2-4. Example air movement table

PICKUP ZONE DIAGRAM

2-36. The PZ diagram (Figure 2-5) graphically depicts the PZ. Units should prepare a separate diagram for each PZ.

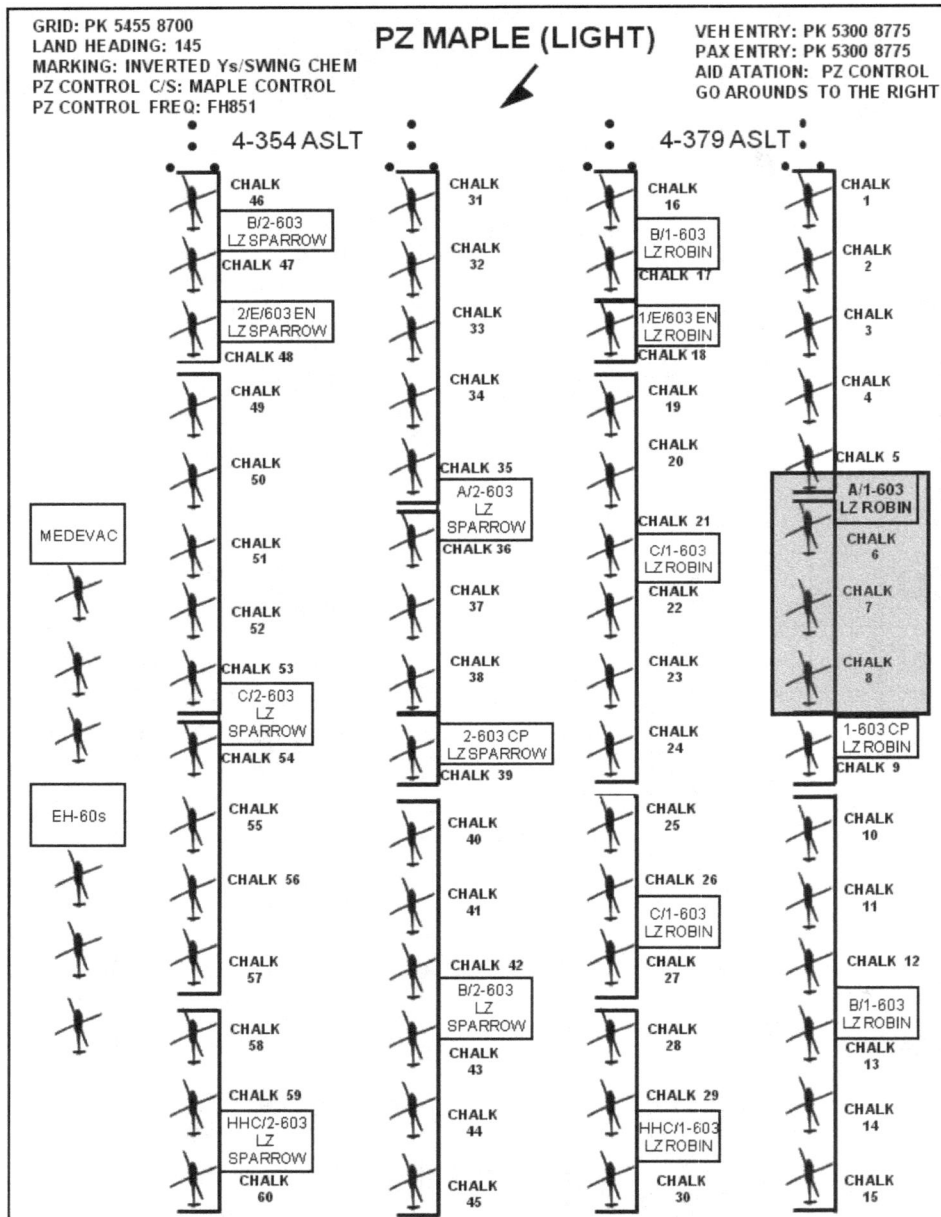

Figure 2-5. Example pickup zone diagram

LANDING ZONE DIAGRAM

2-37. The LZ diagram (Figure 2-6) graphically depicts the LZ. Units should prepare a separate diagram for each LZ.

NAME	GRID	LAND HEADING
ROBIN	**PJ 8850 8515**	**112**
FORMATION	GO AROUND	OBSTACLES/HAZARDS
TRAIL	**RIGHT**	**10m TREES 360^0**
PAX EXIT	OBJ DIR / DIST	ALTERNATE LZ
LEFT & RIGHT	**LANDING ON OBJ**	**CONDOR**
USING UNIT CS/FREQ	WEAPONS STATUS	ADA THREAT DIR/DIST
LEADER / 36.95	**TIGHT**	**UNK**
MARKINGS	DEPARTURE HEADING	ADDITIONAL REMARKS
NONE	**100**	

Figure 2-6. Example landing zone diagram

OPERATIONS KNEEBOARD SKETCH

2-38. An operations kneeboard sketch (Figure 2-7) provided by each Infantry battalion S-3 describes the scheme of maneuver. These concept sketches are given to the aviation S-3 at the BCT rehearsal. Each pilot carries an operations kneeboard sketch to provide situational awareness and to counter the potential for fratricide during close combat operations. These sketches are also included as enclosures to the AMB.

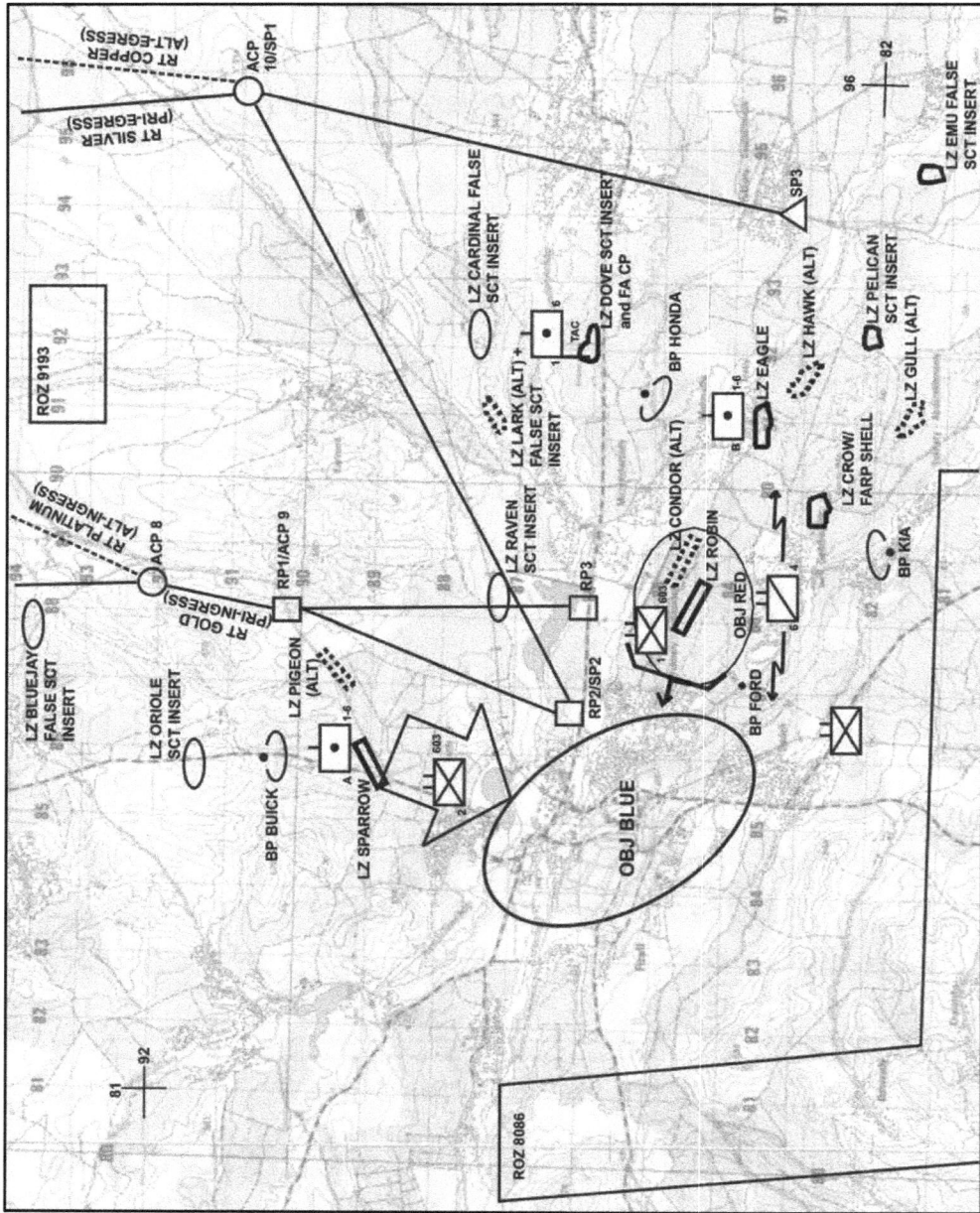

Figure 2-7. Example operations kneeboard sketch

COMMUNICATIONS CARD

2-39. The communications card (Figure 2-8) includes a summary of all call signs and nets.

Net	Call Sign	Net ID	CUE FREQ	Element	Expander	BFT URN	CELL PHONE GSM, IRIDIUM THURAYA
DIV FM1	EAGLE	300	85	CDR	O6	EAGLE 6 101	555-555-5555
DIV FM2		302	39.25	XO	O5	EAGLE 5 101	222-444-3333
BDE CMD	ROCK	350	83.45	S-1	O1	ROCK 01 3-101	111-222-3333
BDE RTS		351	63.95	S-2	O2	ROCK 02 3-101	666-777-8888
BDE O&I		352	86.3	S-3	O3	ROCK 03 3-101	222-333-5555
BDE A/L		353	86.8	S-3 AIR	O3 AIR	ROCK 03 AIR 3-101	999-888-7777
CAN 01		354	83.95	S-4	O4	ROCK 04 3-101	333-555-7777
PZ CNTRL (HEAVY)		355	48.95	S-5	O8	ROCK 08 3-101	888-999-1111
PZ CNTRL (LIGHT)		356	50.95				
PZ VHF TX		VHF TX	143.2875	CSM/1SG	O7	ROCK 07 3-101	444-666-2222
PZ VHF RX		VHF RX	141.0375	CHEMO	11	ROCK 11 3-101	555-888-9999
BDE HF PRI		HF	4.52	SIGO	O9	ROCK 09 3-101	333-222-1111
BDE HF ALT		HF	26.5485	TOC	MAIN	ROCK MAIN 3-101	777-444-2222
ABN 01		UHF	232.3	TAC	TAC	ROCK TAC 3-101	444-555-1111
1-603 IN	LEADER	500	36.95	ALOC	REAR	LEADER REAR 1-187	777-333-2222
2-603 IN	IRON	416	84.75	ENG	13	IRON 13 3-187	999-999-9999
6-4 CAV	WARRIOR	532	60.45	ALO	40	WAR 40 1-33	666-666-5555

Figure 2-8. Example communications card

ROUTE CARDS

2-40. Route cards (Figure 2-9) depict ingress and egress routes on the air assault.

Route Card	Primary Ingress					
Route	GOLD (LZ ROBIN)					
ACP	Grid	Magnetic (MAG) Heading	ETA/ Elapsed	Distance (km)	A/S (knots)	Remarks
PZ	PK 5455 8700					Adjacent to Airfield
SP1	PK 5720 7855	166	04:19 04:19	8.0	60	Base of ridge/beginning of road crossing stream
1	PK 6080 6755	159	04:51 09:10	12.0	80	Major road junction
2	PK 7180 4575	150	09:43 18:53	24.0	80	Major road junction
3	PK 8250 3000	146	08:30 27:23	21.0	80	Road crossing river
4	PK 8770 2150	144	04:03 31:26	9.9	80	Two roads bending towards each other
5	PK 8890 1655	163	02:13 33:39	5.5	80	Road intersection
6	PK 8790 0650	183	04:27 38:06	11.0	80	Saddle
7	PK 8870 0010	171	02:37 40:43	6.5	80	Western slope of hill
8	PJ 8870 9225	175	03:11 43:53	7.9	80	Road junction
9	PJ 8845 9040	188	00:48 44:41	2.0	80	Bend in road
RP2	PJ 8710 8665	196	01:37 46:18	4.0	80	Western edge of lake
LZ Robin	PJ 8850 8510	112	01:20 47:38	2.5	60	North side of airfield
ALT LZ Condor	PJ 8930 8545	118	01:20	2.5	60	Open area north of airfield

Figure 2-9. Sample route card

EXECUTION CHECKLIST

2-41. The air assault execution checklist (Figure 2-10) permits brief, informative radio transmissions on crowded radio nets.

Line #	Time H/Local	Event	M/X	NET	From	To	Code Word
10	H–8+00.00	INITIAL WEATHER CALL	M	BDE CMD	BDE TOC	ALL	
15	4+00:00	INTEL UPDATE/ FINAL WEATHER CALL (INTEL TENT)					
20	3+20:00	C2 AIRCRAFT ARRIVES AT PZ	M	CAN2	PHANTOM	WINGS BAE	ADKINSVILLE
25	3+00:00	1-78 ATK ON STATION	M	CAN1	BEAST 6	ROCK 6	ALBANY
30	3+00:00	5-78 ATK ON STATION	M	CAN1	VARSITY 6	ROCK 6	ABILIENE
35	3+00:00	EH-60 ARRIVES PZ MAPLE	M	CAN1	QUICK FIX	WINGS 6	ALLENTOWN
40	3+00:00	PZ POSTURE OAK					
45	2+55:00	MEDEVAC ARRIVES AT PZ MAPLE	M	CAN1	DUST-OFF 44	WINGS 6	ARLINGTON
50	2+53:00	CDR's COMMUNICATIONS CHECK	M	BDE CMD, CAN1 ABN, OF 1	ROCK 6	GUIDONS	SEE COMMO CARD
55	2+40:00	EH-60S ON STATION ROZ 9889	M	ABN/ CAN1	QUICKFIX 6	WINGS 6 / ROCK 6	ALBION
60	2+44:00	UAS ON STATION ROZ 8086	M	ABN/ CAN1	NIGHTHAWK 6	WINGS 6 / ROCK 6	ASHVILLE
65	2+25:00	5-78 ATK CONDITIONS CALL ON LZ CROW	M	CAN1	VARSITY 6	ROCK 6	CHERRY/ICE CROW
70	2+20:00	5-78 ATK CONDITIONS CALL ON LZ EAGLE	M	CAN1	VARSITY 6	ROCK 6	CHERRY/ICE EAGLE
75	2+15:00	1-78 ATK CONDITIONS CALL ON LZ ROBIN	M	CAN1	BEAST 6	ROCK 6	CHERRY/ICE ROBIN
80	2+10:00	1-78 ATK CONDITIONS CALL ON LZ SPARROW	M	CAN1	BEAST 6	ROCK 6	CHERRY/ICE SPARROW
83	2+05:00	5-78 ATK CONDITIONS CALL ON LZ DOVE	M	CAN1	VARSITY 6	ROCK 6	CHERRY/ICE DOVE
85	2+00:00	PZ POSTURE MAPLE					
90	50:00	MEDEVAC IN ROZ 9193 (1 X UH60V)	M	ABN/ CAN1	DUST-OFF 44 / WINGS 6	WINGS 6 / ROCK 6	ATLANTA
95	44:21	LIFT 1 SER 1 AT SP FOR LZ CROW (A/6-4CAV) (5 X CH47)	M	ABN/ CAN1	PHANTOM 16	WINGS 6 / ROCK 6	AUGUSTA
100	43:21	LIFT 1 SER 2 AT SP FOR LZ CROW (A/6-4CAV) (4 X CH47)	M	ABN/ CAN1	PHANTOM 26	WINGS 06 / ROCK 6	BALTIMORE
105	42:21	LIFT 1 SER 3 AT SP FOR LZ CROW [C/6-4CAV (-)] (3 X CH47)	M	ABN/ CAN1	PHANTOM 36	WINGS 6 / ROCK 6	BANGOR
110	40:21	LIFT 2, SER 1 AT SP FOR LZ ROBIN (A/1-603 IN) (5 X UH-60)	M	ABN/ CAN1	COMANCHERO 16	WINGS 6 / ROCK 6	BOSTON
115	39:21	LIFT 2, SER 2 AT SP FOR LZ ROBIN (A/1-603 IN & HHC/1-603) (4 X UH-60)	M	ABN/ CAN1	COMANCHERO 26	WINGS 6 / ROCK 6	BIRMINGHAM

Figure 2-10. Example execution checklist

AIR ASSAULT TASK FORCE REHEARSAL

2-42. The AATF rehearsal is the culmination of the formal air assault planning process. It is a rehearsal of the entire air assault mission, beginning with condition setting and ending with the commander's expressed end state.

2-43. The rehearsal includes the aviation flight lead, S-3, the AATF staff, and other key leaders. The focus is on the synchronization of all units supporting and executing the air assault. Included in the rehearsal is a discussion and demonstration of likely ground and air contingencies, such as downed aircraft, alternate route or LZ activation, delays in the PZ, alternate SEAD plan, and others suited to a particular mission.

2-44. It is critical that air assault security forces from attack reconnaissance units are represented at the rehearsal to confirm air route deconfliction, fire control measures, and locations of expected attack-by-fire or battle positions. Additionally, the AATF S-3 and FSO, or their designated representatives, attend the rehearsal to brief the ground tactical and FS plans.

AIRCREW BRIEF

2-45. In the aircrew brief, aviation unit and serial commanders brief all flight crews executing the air assault mission. The aircrew brief covers all essential flight crew actions and aviation planning necessary to successfully accomplish the mission. Flight crews must fully understand the mission to execute the air assault successfully.

2-46. The aircrew brief is normally conducted at the aviation battalion level, with the aircrews from each unit in attendance. The aircrew brief can also be conducted at the aviation company level (with assistance from the aviation brigade staff) when mission variables do not allow the brief to be conducted at the battalion level.

AVIATION TASK FORCE REHEARSAL

2-47. The aviation task force rehearsal is similar to the AATF rehearsal. However, its focus is the aviation scheme of maneuver and the contingencies associated with the movement of aircraft and how they apply to the mission. The purpose of the aviation task force rehearsal is to validate synchronization.

2-48. At a minimum, the rehearsal includes the pilot in command of each aircraft, the AMC of each serial, the aviation task force S-3, and the aviation task force commander. Additional requirements are set by the AMC. Topics discussed should include, but are not limited to, route deconfliction, bump plan execution, execution matrix, downed aircraft recovery procedures, personnel recovery, actions on contact, and PZ and LZ procedures.

> *Note.* Based on the mission timeline, attack reconnaissance units may not be able to be fully represented at the rehearsal. Often, attack reconnaissance units have already begun shaping operations that support the air assault operation.

SECTION V – SHAPING OPERATIONS

2-49. Successful execution of an air assault may be decisive to accomplishing a given mission, but it is not necessarily the decisive operation. Air assaults are often conducted as shaping operations to establish the conditions for the decisive operation through the effects rendered on the enemy and terrain. A shaping operation is an operation at any echelon that creates and preserves conditions for the success of the decisive operation. An example of this is a company conducting an air assault to seize a bridge and secure a crossing site in support of a deliberate combined arms battalion-level attack that requires the bridge as a crossing site. (See FM 3-0 for details.)

2-50. Similarly, the AATF sets the conditions for a successful air assault by conducting shaping operations of its own. The AATFC may employ ground and air reconnaissance units, attack aviation units, UASs, close air support, and lethal artillery fires in order to conduct shaping operations to limit or mitigate the tactical risk to a minimal or acceptable level for execution of the air assault.

PLANNING CONSIDERATIONS

2-51. The AATFC determines the exact conditions that must be created and preserved in accordance with the mission variables and the degree of acceptable tactical risk associated with each air assault. When determining these conditions, he considers the following factors:

- Shaping operations are not limited to conducting ground and air reconnaissance, SEAD, and preparatory fires. They may require additional augmentation from higher headquarters, the supporting aviation unit, and the supported unit staffs in order to succeed.
- Assessing the effects of lethal fires by conducting battle damage assessment (BDA) of enemy forces and capabilities is not easy. Enemies often remove wounded or dead personnel and equipment to make friendly BDA more difficult and less accurate. In weighing the validity of BDA projections, it is important to balance confirmed intelligence against friendly combat power applied. More combat power may be useful against uncertain BDA.
- The threat, the ability to assess the impact of shaping operations, and the air assault execution time may determine the duration of shaping operations. Allocate as much time as possible.

2-52. Conducting shaping operations to create and preserve the proper conditions for air assault execution is an iterative process. Based on his situational understanding, the AATFC decides what part of the situation must change to ensure the success of the air assault. The commander directs available reconnaissance and surveillance units to detect the location of enemy systems that unacceptably endanger the air assault's success. This allows lethal and nonlethal systems, such as artillery, jammers, attack reconnaissance aircraft, and UASs, to target and deliver the desired fires and effects against those enemy systems prior to launch.

2-53. The AATF staffs continue to plan and prepare for the air assault. The AATFC considers employing service and joint fires, if available, to help set the conditions. The commander requests assistance from higher headquarters if sufficient organic assets and information are not available to accomplish the mission. The commander then assesses the progress of the shaping operations. This process repeats until the commander is satisfied with the result or operational necessity forces him to either abort or conduct the air assault.

CONDITION CHECKS

2-54. Condition checks are coordination meetings held by the AATF staff to update the AATFC on the status of how well shaping operations are creating the conditions to execute the air assault. The conditions that must exist for air assault execution must be continuously monitored. It is important to consider the latency of the information when presenting it to the commander for a decision.

2-55. The initial air assault condition check is usually held in the AATF or ground tactical force main CP. All air assault staff principals are represented. Brigade combat team and higher headquarter liaison officers attend each other's condition checks in person when possible and by video-teleconference or conference call when necessary. The final condition check is usually held near the air assault task force's PZ control CP. It includes a review of the latest friendly, terrain and weather, and enemy situations.

2-56. An air assault condition check considers critical factors to evaluate in order to recommend the execution of an air assault. For example, air assaults planned for dawn and dusk periods are extremely dependant on weather and visibility. Air assaults planned for these periods increase the risks to air assets. The S-2 evaluates the weather and visibility conditions and recommends to the AATFC his assessment of those conditions in regards to the execution of the air assault.

2-57. Figure 2-11 lists examples of factors to evaluate during a condition check. These factors provide the basis for the air assault staff to recommend a (go), abort (no-go), or delay decision to the AATFC.

Note. Following the checklist does not equal setting the conditions. Once variables are confirmed and options are considered, an informed go or no-go decision can be made.

Weather
Warfighting Functions Check
> Intelligence.
> Movement and Maneuver.
> Fires.
> Protection.
> Sustainment.
> Command and Control.

AATFC Recommendation: (Go, No-Go, Delay)
> Intelligence: (G-2/S-2).
> - Current weather and light data for air assault and close air support.
> - Post air assault weather.
> - Suitability of LZs.
> - Enemy C2 warfare capabilities identified.
> - Enemy indirect fire in range of primary and alternate LZs.
> - Enemy direct fire in range of primary and alternate LZs.
> - Enemy wheel, mechanized, or armor force able to influence primary or alternate LZs.
> - BDA Confidence Level (focus on air defense artillery and other key weapons).
> - Eyes on key named areas of interest with communications to shooter.
> - Higher headquarters priority of higher collection effort.

> Movement and Maneuver: (G-3/S-3, G-3 AVN/BAO).
> - Assault aircraft and crews ready.
> - Attack aviation ready.
> - Sufficient lifts available for minimum force requirements.
> - C2 warfare operations coordinated within limits of the rules of engagement.
> - PZs ready and secure.
> - Units in PZ posture.
> - Personnel recovery and combat search and rescue in place.
> - Primary and alternate LZs designated and rehearsed.
> - Higher and adjacent units notified of plan and assets available to reinforce and support operations.
> - Antifratricide measures in place.
> - Plan for civilians on the battlefield.
>   - LZ obstacle clearing teams ready.
>   - Flight landing strip clearing team ready.
>   - Flight landing strip layout confirmed.
>   - Airfield repair package ready for airdrop.
>   - Countermobility assets in place to support.
>   - Ground assault planned and in progress.

> Fires: (FSO/Fires Cell).
> - Joint SEAD and intelligence and electronic warfare coordination complete.
> - Fire support coordinating measures coordinated.
> - Firing units in position.
> - SEAD fires planned on suspected locations/fire plans forwarded to subordinate units.
> - Close air support coordinated and available.
> - Appropriate communications established.
> - Counterfire radar coverage in place and planned.
> - Tactical air control party task organized.
> - Fire plan rehearsed.
> - Air assault on air tasking order.
> - Nonlethal SEAD covers critical portions of operation.
> - Enemy C2 warfare suppression plan.
> - Known fire support assets within range of primary and alternate LZs destroyed and suppressed; SEAD fires planned on suspected locations.
> - Passage points covered by indirect fire.

Figure 2-11. Example air assault condition check format

Protection: (G-3 AVN/BAE, DIV/BDE ENG, CBRN Section).

- Routes, ROZs and mission on ACO and air tasking order.
- Coordinated friendly & cross boundary air defense artillery locations and coverage.
- Early warning coverage for artillery raid LZs.
- Joint Tactical Information Distribution System located with assault.
- Air defense coverage of critical nodes (PZ, AVN assembly area, FARP).
- Weapons control status – hold along air routes.
- Route clearance and survivability assets confirmed.
- LZs not contaminated.
- Obstacles and barrier plan in place for engagement area shaping.
- Decontamination assets available and coordinated.

Sustainment: (G-3 AVN/BAO, G-4/S-4).

- FARP(s) ready to support mission.
  - Primary FARP.
  - Alternate FARP.
- Sufficient supplies ready.
  - Class I/Water.
  - Class III.
  - Class IV.
  - Class V.
  - Class VIII.
- Availability of alternate FARP.
- Medical and casualty evacuation planned and ready.
- Downed aircraft recovery team/maintenance plan/assets ready.
- Essential transportation plan and assets ready.

Command and Control: (G-3/S-3, G-6/S-6).

- Seats out risk management completed and approved.
- Appropriate C2 element in PZ posture.
- Tactical satellite channel available.
- High frequency channel available.
- Retrans in place (if required).
- Nonsecure/Secure Internet Protocol Router package available.
- All preparation for Joint Network Node mission support complete.
- Execution checklist complete and distributed.
- LNO teams to higher and adjacent in place and aware of plan.
- Media plan in place.
- Rehearsals complete.
- Commo rehearsals complete (to include C2 aircraft).

LEGEND	
Green	Planned, In Progress, or Low Risk
Yellow	Delayed, Degraded, or Moderate Risk
Red	Not Identified or High Risk
Black	Extremely High Risk
White	N/A

Figure 2-11. Example air assault condition check format (continued)

SECTION VI – ABORT CRITERIA

2-58. The methodology used in executing an air assault involves setting the conditions, providing suppressive fires immediately before and on landing, and continuously monitoring abort criteria from beginning to end.

2-59. Abort criteria are important considerations when a change of one or more conditions in the objective area or LZ seriously threatens mission success. As such, they are the friendly force information requirement relating to any ongoing air assault operation and requiring command consideration regarding mission continuation. It is important that the AMB clearly defines abort criteria and that the AATFC monitors them throughout the operation.

2-60. If an abort criterion is met, a decision sequence is used prior to aborting the mission:

- **Delay.** If time is available, a mission can be delayed to correct a circumstance that may abort a mission and set the conditions.
- **Divert.** If time is not available or a delay will not correct an abort criterion, the task force may execute a divert contingency.
- **Abort.** If an abort criterion exists and a delay or diversion to the mission will not correct it, the mission can be aborted by the AATFC.
  - A lift is aborted when it reaches an abort criterion. The mission itself is not aborted.
  - A mission is aborted when an abort criterion exists for the entire mission and the AATFC decides to abort.

2-61. Given the continued advantage of using the primary LZ over the alternate, delay while en route or at the PZ is preferable to diverting. The AATFC must evaluate the risk of such a delay in light of time, fuel, enemy, and other mission variables.

2-62. Planners establish proposed abort criteria to assist commanders in deciding when success of the operation is no longer probable. The AATFC retains authority for abort decisions. The six factors that determine abort criteria for air assault missions are—

- **Weather.** Adverse weather conditions make flying unsafe and degrade the effectiveness of the helicopter's organic weapon systems. AR 95-1 sets the minimum weather conditions, stated as a ceiling and visibility, for certain types of helicopter missions over certain types of terrain. Based on a recommendation from the AMC, the AATFC decides to abort the mission or execute as planned. Weather conditions must be at or above minimums for the entire estimated time aircraft are flying and over the entire area in which they operate through 1 hour after planned mission completion unless waived by the higher headquarters due to criticality of a specific combat operation.
- **Available aircraft.** The ground tactical plan for an air assault operation depends on the rapid massing of combat power at the critical place and time by helicopters. Aviation battalions report mission capable rates for planning purposes. If actual mission capable rates fall below the planning figure, the AATF is unable to build its combat power as quickly as planned.
- **Time.** This refers most particularly to light and darkness. United States armed forces gain a significant advantage over most military forces in the world by operating at night. Unsophisticated air defense systems rely on visual target tracking and acquisition. Also, some aircraft are more vulnerable during daylight hours due to size or speed, such as the CH-47. Abort criteria in terms of takeoff times are established to ensure fighter management and aircraft survivability.
- **Mission essential combat power.** Air assault mission planners use mission variables to determine the minimum combat power (including Infantry, artillery, and attack helicopters) necessary to ensure mission success. Abort criteria are used to ensure that friendly forces have the required combat ratio for the operation.
- **Mission criticality.** The success of units and future operations may depend on the success of the air assault mission. Therefore, some air assault operations may proceed despite the presence of circumstances that would normally abort the mission.
- **Enemy.** Certain types of enemy activity, especially along air routes or in the vicinity of LZs or objectives, may abort an air assault mission. Abort criteria are usually stated in terms of the size or type of an enemy unit, the type of enemy equipment (especially air defense), and the proximity of the enemy to present or future friendly locations.

Chapter 3

Ground Tactical Plan

The ground tactical plan is the foundation of a successful air assault on which all other air assault planning stages are based. It is the decisive operation for the air AATF because it accomplishes the mission assigned by the higher headquarters. It specifies actions in the objective area that lead to accomplishment of the mission and subsequent operations.

SECTION I – ELEMENTS

3-1. The ground tactical plan may assume a variety of possibilities depending on the commander's evaluation of the mission variables. The ground tactical plan for an air assault contains essentially the same elements as any other terrain- or enemy-oriented offensive operation. However, the elements of the ground tactical plan are prepared to capitalize on speed and mobility to achieve surprise. The following elements are critical to the planning process.

TASK ORGANIZATION

3-2. When determining the task force organization, air assault planners emphasize—

- Maximizing combat power in the assault to heighten the surprise and shock effect, which is especially important if the AATF plans to land on or near the objective. Assaulting forces organize on or near the objective—prepared to rapidly eliminate enemy forces, immediately seize objectives, and rapidly consolidate for subsequent operations.
- Ensuring the task force inserts enough force to accomplish initial objectives quickly. To prevent being defeated by repositioning mobile enemy forces, air assault task forces must be massed in the LZ to build up a significant early combat power capability. If adequate combat power cannot be introduced quickly into the objective area, the air assault force lands away from the objective to build up combat power and then assaults like any other combat unit.
- Ensuring the AATFC properly allocates his logistics assets to sustain the task force until follow-on forces arrive.

MISSION STATEMENT

3-3. The mission is the task, together with the purpose, that clearly indicates the action to be taken and the reason therefore (JP 1-02). Commanders analyze a mission in terms of the commander's intent two echelons up, specified tasks, and implied tasks. They also consider the mission of adjacent units to understand how they contribute to the decisive operation of their higher headquarters. This analysis produces the unit's mission statement.

3-4. A mission statement is a short sentence or paragraph that describes the organization's essential task (or tasks) and purpose—a clear statement of the action to be taken and the reason for doing so. The mission statement contains the elements of who, what, when, where, and why, but seldom specifies how (JP 5-0).

3-5. It is important to remember that an air assault is a type of operation and not a tactical mission task. (See FM 3-90 for details on tactical mission tasks.) Figure 3-1 provides an example of a mission statement for a unit conducting and air assault.

COMMANDER'S INTENT

3-6. It is critical that the AATF planners receive the commander's intent as soon as possible after the mission is received. Even if the ground tactical plan is not complete, air assault planning often begins after the AATFC issues his intent.

3-7. The commander's intent is a clear, concise statement of what the force must do and the conditions the force must establish with respect to the enemy, terrain, and civilian considerations that represent the desired end state (FM 3-0). The commander's intent describes what constitutes success in an operation. It includes the purpose of the operations and the conditions that define the end state. The commander's intent links the mission, concept of operations, and tasks to subordinates.

CONCEPT OF OPERATIONS

3-8. The concept of operations is a statement that directs the manner in which subordinate units cooperate to accomplish the mission and establishes the sequence of actions the force will use to achieve the end state. It is normally expressed in terms of decisive, shaping, and sustaining operations (FM 3-0). The concept of operations expands on the mission statement and commander's intent by describing how and in what sequence the commander wants the force to accomplish the mission.

3-9. Commanders identify the decisive operation and unit(s) responsible for conducting the decisive operation. This allows them to articulate their shaping operations and the principal task of the units assigned each shaping operation. Commanders complete their concept of operations with sustaining actions essential to the success of decisive and shaping operations.

DECISIVE OPERATIONS

3-10. The decisive operation is the operation that directly accomplishes the mission. It determines the outcome of a major operation, battle, or engagement (FM 3-0). The decisive operation is the focal point around which commanders design the entire operation.

3-11. In Figure 3-1, the unit has been directed by its higher headquarters to conduct an air assault to destroy enemy forces on Objective Horse. The AATFC determines that his decisive operation is the attack to destroy enemy forces on Objective Horse. He further decides that the decisive point of this operation is the successful air assault of his forces into the objective area to destroy the enemy.

SHAPING OPERATIONS

3-12. A shaping operation is an operation at any echelon that creates and preserves conditions for the success of the decisive operation (FM 3-0). Shaping operations establish conditions for the decisive operation through effects on the enemy, population, and terrain.

3-13. In Figure 3-1, the AATFC employs his reconnaissance units (to include scouts, CBRN platoon, and UAS) to conduct reconnaissance and surveillance of proposed LZs and the objective area in order to identify and target enemy forces near the LZs and objective vicinities. The fires battalion is positioned to provide lethal fires throughout all phases of the operation. It is prepared to deny the enemy's ability to conduct reconnaissance, defeat his strike operations, and neutralize his ability to communicate and command. The supporting aviation unit is prepared to conduct reconnaissance in coordination with the reconnaissance unit or provide lethal fires to neutralize or destroy enemy forces in the objective area once they have been identified. The commander also considers employing other enablers that may not be in his task force, such as close air support and electronic warfare assets. The purpose of these operations is to set and preserve the conditions on the LZ and objective area that allow the maneuver forces to launch the air assault and execute a successful attack to destroy the enemy on the objective.

SUSTAINING OPERATIONS

3-14. A sustaining operation is an operation at any echelon that enables the decisive operation or shaping operations by generating and maintaining combat power (FM 3-0).

3-15. The AATFC considers how he will refuel the supporting aviation unit and resupply and provide responsive medical and casualty evacuation to his task force. He determines that this operation may require bringing a forward logistics element from the brigade support battalion (BSB) and some of its crucial elements forward to conduct casualty evacuation, resupply, and equipment recovery. He also positions a forward medical team with a maneuver unit to treat casualties prior to evacuation to a medical treatment facility.

TASKS TO SUBORDINATE UNITS

3-16. Tasks to subordinate units direct individual units to perform specific tasks. A task is a clearly defined and measurable activity accomplished by individuals and organizations (FM 7-0). Tasks are specific activities that contribute to accomplishing missions or other requirements. Tasks direct friendly action. The purpose of each task should nest with completing another task, achieving an objective, or attaining an end state condition.

3-17. Examples of decisive, shaping, and sustaining activities in Figure 3-1 are—

- **Movement and maneuver.** Maneuver units conduct an air assault and attack to destroy enemy forces on objectives. Aviation units conduct air insertion of reconnaissance elements near the objective area and provide interdiction and CCA against identified enemy forces in the objective area.
- **Intelligence.** Reconnaissance units conduct reconnaissance and surveillance of LZs and the objective area to identify enemy forces for targeting by fires and aviation assets in order to set conditions for air assault execution.
- **Fires.** Fires battalion provides lethal fires on identified enemy positions on or near LZs and the objective to neutralize enemy forces and help set conditions for air assault execution.
- **Sustainment.** The BSB refuels aviation assets during air operations and establishes a forward medical treatment point colocated with maneuver unit.
- **Command and control.** The AATFC deploys in a C2 aircraft to provide C2 oversight of the mission.

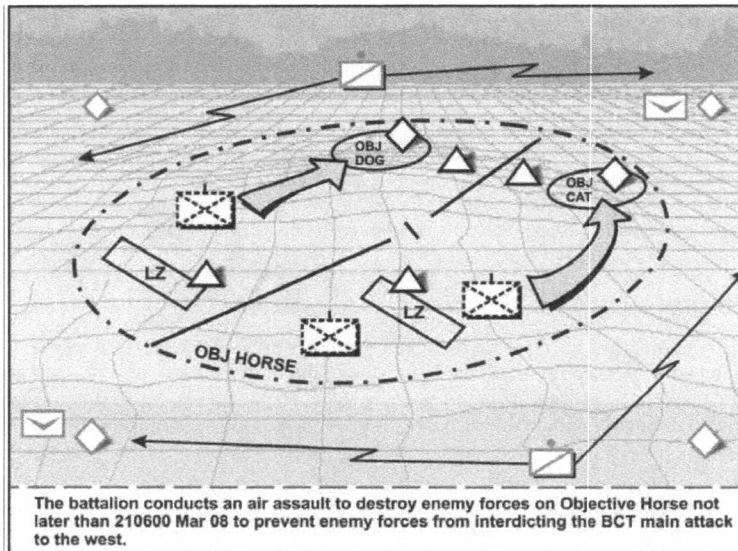

The battalion conducts an air assault to destroy enemy forces on Objective Horse not later than 210600 Mar 08 to prevent enemy forces from interdicting the BCT main attack to the west.

Figure 3-1. Battlefield organization

SECTION II – AIR-GROUND INTEGRATION

3-18. Aviation and ground units require effective integration and synchronization to conduct air assaults successfully and minimize the potential for fratricide and civilian casualties. When used in conjunction with ground forces, fires from the attack reconnaissance aviation, Air Force close air support, and employment of UASs provide tremendous advantages to ground forces in contact. Effective integration of air and ground units begins at the AATF and continues down to the lowest unit level. In an air assault, the AATF plans and coordinates with the supporting CAB through their AVN LNO and the ADAM/BAE to support the ground tactical plan. Integration should start at the home station with implementation of effective standing operating procedures, habitual relationships, and training if possible. It continues through planning, preparation, and execution of the air assault (FM 3-04.111).

3-19. To ensure effective integration, air assault commanders and staffs should consider some fundamentals for air-ground integration. The following fundamentals provide a framework for enhancing the effectiveness of both air and ground maneuver units:

- Understanding capabilities and limitations of each force.
- Using standing operating procedures.
- Habitual relationships.
- Regular training events.
- C2.
- Maximizing and concentrating effects of available assets.
- Employment methods.
- Synchronization.

3-20. Synchronization involves merging the air and ground fights into one to properly apply aviation capabilities in accordance with the supported AATFCs intent. Synchronization ideally begins early in the planning process with the involvement of the ADAM/BAE. The ADAM/BAE advises the AATFC on aviation capabilities and the best way to use aviation to support mission objectives. Ensuring the aviation liaison officer AVN LNO or BAE passes along the task and purpose for aviation support and continually provides updates as needed is of equal importance. Simply stated, ensuring the aviation brigade and subordinate unit staffs fully understand the AATF scheme of maneuver and commander's intent is critical to successful air-ground integration. (See FM 3-04.111 for details.)

3-21. Employing attack reconnaissance aviation with ground maneuver forces requires coordinated force-oriented control measures and the CCA brief allowing aviation forces to support ground maneuver with direct fires while minimizing fratricide risks. Aviation liaison officers should identify early in the planning process the minimum AATF graphics required for operations (boundaries, phase lines, attack-by-fire positions, objectives, and so on). Brigade aviation element and liaison officer personnel should also ensure that supported units are familiar with CCA request procedures and marking techniques. (See FM 3-04.126 for details.)

CLOSE COMBAT ATTACKS

3-22. A CCA is a coordinated hasty or deliberate attack by attack reconnaissance aviation aircraft against enemy forces that are in close proximity to friendly forces engaged in close combat. In most instances, the attack aviation may already occupy holding areas, battle or support-by-fire positions or are in overwatch of the ground unit as it begins its assault. The AATF employs CCA procedures to ensure that these aviation fires destroy the enemy with minimal risk to friendly forces (See FM 3-04.126).

3-23. The most important factor of successful CCAs is positive and direct communication between aviation and ground elements. Aviators and ground elements need to understand the following procedures to successfully employ CCA.

CLOSE COMBAT ATTACK REQUEST

3-24. Any element in contact uses the CCA brief to initiate the CCA. The CCA brief allows the ground maneuver forces to communicate and reconfirm to the aircraft the exact location of friendly and enemy forces. Figure 3-2 shows the general CCA request procedure. The procedure remains the same regardless of the type of unit in contact or the responding aviation element. The ground commander owning the terrain clears fires during the CCA by giving aircrews the situational awareness of the location of friendly elements. The ground commander also deconflicts the airspace between any indirect fires, close air support, and the CCA aircraft.

3-25. After receiving the request for CCA, the aircrew informs the ground unit leader of the battle position, attack- or support-by-fire position (or series of positions) the team is occupying, and the location from which the attack aircraft will engage the enemy with direct fire. The size of this position varies depending on the number of aircraft using the position, the size of the engagement area, and the type of terrain. The position must be close enough to the requesting unit to facilitate efficient target handover. Aircraft leaders normally offset the position from the flank of the friendly ground position. This helps to ensure that rotor wash, ammunition casing expenditure, and the general signature of the aircraft do not interfere with operations on the ground. The offset position allows the aircraft to engage the enemy on his flanks rather than his front. It also reduces the risk of fratricide along the helicopter gun-target line.

Format 12. Close Combat Attack Briefing – Ground to Air (5-Line)
1. Observer / Warning Order "_____, this is _____, Fire Mission, Over"   (Aircraft Call Sign)   (Observer Call Sign)
2. Friendly Location / Mark "**My position** _____, **marked by** _____"   (TRP, Grid, etc.)   (Strobe, Beacon, IR Strobe, etc.)
3. Target Location "**Target Location** _____"   (Bearing [magnetic] and Range [meters], TRP, Grid, etc.)
4. Target Description / Mark "_____, **marked by** _____"   (Target Description)   (IR Pointer, Tracer, etc.)
5. Remarks (Threats, Danger Close Clearance, Restriction, At My Command, etc.) **"Over"**
AS REQUIRED: **1.** Clearance: Transmission of the 5-Line CCA Brief is clearance to fire (unless danger close.) For closer fire, the observer/commander must accept responsibility for increased risk. State "Cleared Danger Close" in line 5. This clearance may be preplanned. **2.** At My Command: For positive control of the aircraft, state **"At My Command"** on line 5. The aircraft will call **"Ready for Fire"** when ready.

Figure 3-2. Close combat attack request procedure

UNIT AND TARGET MARKING

3-26. Marking techniques for identifying targets and friendly positions vary from one ground unit to another (Table 3-1). The CCA request should include a detailed description of all friendly locations and target locations in relation to friendly positions. It should also include the target description and how it will be marked.

3-27. For mutual protection and clarity on the appropriate target, the ground unit does not mark the target until requested by the aviation element. This in no way restricts the ground unit from returning fire from the enemy. However, the ground unit should consider that the aircrews may not be able to distinguish the correct target from other fires if they mark the target with fire. Ground units should have multiple means of marking their positions. If the target is marked by fire, the aviation element requests the ground unit to stop mark. The aviation element calls when clear of the area and reports estimated BDA.

3-28. The CCA cannot be conducted without positive identification of friendly and enemy forces by both the ground and aviation commander prior to attack aviation aircraft opening fire. The aviation element tailors its attack angles and weapon selections based upon the target and friendly unit proximity to the target.

Table 3-1. Close combat attack friendly unit and target marking

METHOD	DAY	NIGHT	NVG	NVS	FRIENDLY MARKS	TARGET MARKS	REMARKS
Smoke	Go	No Go	Marginal	No Go	Good	Good	Easy ID. May compromise friendly positions, obscure target, or warn of FS employment. Placement may be difficult because of terrain, trees, or structures.
Smoke (IR)	Go	Go	Go	No Go	Good	Good	Easy ID. May compromise friendly positions, obscure target, or warn of FS employment. Placement may be difficult because of terrain, trees, or structures. Night marking is greatly enhanced through use of IR reflective smoke.
Illumination, Ground Burst	Go	Go	Go	No Go	NA	Good	Easy ID. May wash out NVDs.
Signal Mirror	Go	No Go	No Go	No Go	Good	NA	Avoids compromise of friendly location. Depends on weather and available light. May be lost in reflections from other reflective surfaces such as windshields, windows, or water.
Spot Light	No Go	Go	Go	No Go	Good	Marginal	Highly visible to all. Compromises friendly position and warns of FS employment. Effectiveness depends on the degree of ambient lighting.
IR Spot Light	No Go	No Go	Go	No Go	Good	Marginal	Visible to all NVGs. Effectiveness depends on the degree of ambient lighting.
IR Laser Pointer (below .4 watts)	No Go	No Go	Go	No Go	Good	Marginal	Effectiveness depends on the degree of ambient lighting.
IR Laser Pointer (above .4 watts)	No Go	No Go	Go	No Go	Good	Good	Less affected by ambient light and weather conditions. Highly effective under all but the most highly lit or worst weather conditions. IZLID-2 is the curent example.
Visual Laser	No Go	Go	Go	No Go	Good	Marginal	Highly visible to all. High risk of compromise. Effective, depending upon degree of ambient light.
Laser Designator	Go	Go	No Go	Go	NA	Good	Highly effective with precision-guided munitions. Very restrictive laser-acquisition cone and requires LOS to target. May require precoord-ination of laser codes. Requires PGM or LST equipped.
Electronic Beacon	NA	NA	NA	NA	Excellent	Good	Ideal friendly marking for AC-130 and some USAF CAS. Not compatible with Navy/Marines. Can be used as a TRP. Coordination with aircrew essential.

Table 3-1. Close combat attack friendly unit and target marking (continued)

METHOD	DAY	NIGHT	NVG	NVS	FRIENDLY MARKS	TARGET MARKS	REMARKS
Tracers	Go	Go	Go	No Go	No Go	Marginal	May compromise position. May be difficult to distinguish mark from other gunfire. During daytime use, may be more effective to kick up dust surrounding target.
VS-17 Panel	Go	No Go	No Go	No Go	Good	NA	Easy to see when visibility is good. Must be shielded from the enemy.
IR Paper	No Go	No Go	No Go	Go	Good	NA	Must be shielded from the enemy. Affected by ambient temperature.
AN/PAQ-4C IR Aiming Light	No Go	No Go	Go	No Go	NA	Good	Effective to about 600 meters.
AN/PEQ-2A IR Aiming Light Pointer, Illuminator	No Go	No Go	Go	No Go	NA	Good	Effective to about 1,300 meters. Can illuminate the target.
Chem Light	No Go	Go	Go	No Go	Good	NA	Must be shielded from enemy enemy observation. Affected by ambient light. Spin to give unique signature.
IR Chem Light	No Go	No Go	Go	No Go	Good	NA	Must be shielded from enemy observation. Affected by ambient light. Spin to give unique signature.
Strobe	No Go	Go	Go	No Go	Excellent	NA	Visible to all. Affected by ambient light.
IR Strobe	No Go	No Go	Go	No Go	Excellent	NA	Effective depends on ambient light. Coded strobes aid acquisition. Visible to all with NVGs.
Flare	Go	Go	Go	Marginal	Excellent	NA	Visible to all. Easily seen by aircrew.
IR Flare	No Go	No Go	Go	No Go	Excellent	NA	Easily seen by aircrews with NVGs.
Glint/IR Panel	No Go	No Go	No Go	Go	Good	NA	Not readily detected by enemy. Effective except in high ambient light.
Combat ID Panel	Go	No Go	No Go	No Go	Good	NA	Provides temperature contrast on vehicles or building.
Chemical Heat Sources, MRE Heater	No Go	No Go	No Go	Go	Poor	NA	Can be lost in thermal clutter. Difficult to acquire. Best to contrast on a cold background.
Briefing Pointer	No Go	Go	Go	No Go	Fair	Poor	Short range.
Hydra 70 Illumination	Go	Go	Go	Go	NA	Good	Assists with direct fire and adjustment of indirect fire.

TARGET HANDOVER

3-29. The rapid and accurate marking of a target is essential to a positive target handover. Aircraft conducting CCAs normally rely on a high rate of speed and low altitude for survivability in the target area. As such, the aircrew generally has an extremely limited amount of time to acquire both the friendly and enemy marks. It is essential that the ground unit has the marking ready and turned on when requested by the aircrew.

3-30. Attack reconnaissance aircrews use both thermal sight and night vision goggles to fly with and acquire targets. After initially engaging the target, the aircrew generally approaches from a different angle for survivability reasons if another attack is required. The observer makes adjustments using the eight cardinal directions and distance (meters) in relation to the last round's impact and the actual target. At the conclusion of the CCA, the aircrew provides their best estimate of BDA to the unit in contact.

BATTLE DAMAGE ASSESSMENT AND REATTACK

3-31. After the attack aircraft complete the requested CCA mission, the aircrew provides a BDA to the ground commander. Based on his intent, the ground maneuver commander determines if another attack is required to achieve his desired end state. The CCA operation can continue until the aircraft have expended all available munitions or fuel. However, if the AMC receives a request for another attack, he must carefully evaluate his ability to extend the operation. If not able, he calls for relief on station by another attack team if available. It is unlikely that the original team will have enough time to refuel, rearm, and return to station.

CLEARANCE OF FIRES

3-32. During an air assault with numerous aircraft in the vicinity of the LZ, it is critical that procedures are in place to deconflict airspace between aircraft and indirect fires, to include—

- Ensure aircrews have the current and planned indirect fire positions (including mortars) supporting the air assault prior to the mission.
- Plan for informal airspace coordinating areas and check firing procedures and communications to ensure artillery and mortars firing from within the LZ do not endanger any subsequent serials landing or departing, CCA, or close air support.
- Ensure at least one of the aviation team members monitors the FS net for situational awareness.
- Advise the aviation element if the location of indirect fire units changes from that planned.
- Ensure all participating units are briefed daily on current ACO or air tasking order changes and updates that may affect air mission planning and execution.
- Ensure all units update firing unit locations, firing point origins, and final protective fire lines as they change for inclusion in current ACO.

3-33. The AATFC or GTC can establish an airspace coordinating area. For example, he can designate that all indirect fires be south of and all aviation stay north of a specified gridline for a specific period of time. This is one technique for deconflicting airspace while allowing both indirect fires and attack aviation to attack the same target. The GTC can then deactivate the informal airspace coordinating area when the situation permits.

CLOSE AIR SUPPORT

3-34. Close air support is air action by fixed- and rotary-wing aircraft against hostile targets that are in close proximity to friendly forces and that require detailed integration of each air mission with the fire and movement of those forces (JP 3-0). Like CCA, close air support can be conducted at any place and time friendly forces are in close proximity to enemy forces based on availability. All leaders in the AATF should understand how to employ close air support to destroy, disrupt, suppress, fix, harass, neutralize, or delay enemy forces. Nomination of close air support targets is the responsibility of the commander, ALO, and S-3 at each level The AATF may receive close air support from Air Force, Navy, Marine Corps, or multinational units.

CAPABILITIES AND EMPLOYMENT

3-35. In some cases, U.S. Air Force aircraft are available to provide close air support. Requests for these aircraft are processed through the tactical air control party colocated with the BCT main CP. The tactical air control party is organized as an air execution cell capable of requesting and executing Type 2 or 3 terminal attack control of close air support missions. The manning of the cell depends on the situation but, at a minimum, includes an ALO and a joint terminal attack controller (JTAC). In order to make a recommendation to the commander regarding the use of close air support aircraft, the leader on the ground should be familiar with the characteristics of the aircraft predominantly used in the close air support role. (See JP 3-09.3 and FM 3-09.32 for details about characteristics and capabilities of fixed-wing aircraft available for close air support.)

BRIEFING FORMAT

3-36. Two types of close air support requests are—

- **Preplanned requests** that may be filled with either scheduled or on-call air missions. Those close air support requirements foreseen early enough to be included in the first air tasking order distribution are submitted as preplanned air support requests for close air support. Only those air support requests submitted in sufficient time to be included in the joint air tasking cycle planning phases and supported on the air tasking order are considered preplanned requests (JP 3-09.3).
- **Immediate requests** that are mostly filled by diverting preplanned missions or with on-call missions. Immediate requests arise from situations that develop outside the air tasking order planning cycle (JP 3-09.3).

3-37. The ALO and JTAC personnel in the tactical air control party are the primary means for requesting and controlling close air support. However, reconnaissance units conducting shaping operations, such as reconnaissance and surveillance missions that have joint fires observer certified personnel, may observe and request CAS through the JTAC. (See FM 3-09.32 or JP 3-09.3 for examples.)

UNMANNED AIRCRAFT SYSTEM OPERATIONS

3-38. Unmanned aircraft system operations provide surveillance capabilities to enhance the AATFCs situational awareness as he plans, coordinates, and executes the air assault. The commander can employ UASs from any of his organic elements or he can request to have direct access to real-time or near-real-time feeds from additional UAS support from his higher headquarters. They are particularly effective when employed together with ground and attack reconnaissance elements as a team during shaping operations in which the commander is trying to create the conditions for successful air assault execution. (See FM 3-04.155 for details.)

CAPABILITIES

3-39. Unmanned aircraft systems bring numerous capabilities to the AATF. Employed with ground and attack reconnaissance units, they provide near-real-time reconnaissance, surveillance, and target acquisition capabilities.

Reconnaissance Operations

3-40. When UASs complement the ground reconnaissance units during reconnaissance operations, they normally operate forward of the element (METT-TC dependent). They can conduct detailed surveillance of areas that are particularly dangerous to ground reconnaissance units, such as LZs and objective areas. They can also be effectively employed in support of operations in urban terrain.

3-41. They can support route reconnaissance forward of reconnaissance units or be employed in conjunction with reconnaissance units when it is necessary to reconnoiter multiple routes simultaneously. The reconnaissance unit leader can employ UASs to support a screen of an area or zone reconnaissance mission. Upon contact, UASs provide early warning for the element and then maintain contact until the element conducts a reconnaissance handover from the UAS to another element.

Security Operations

3-42. In security operations, UASs complement the reconnaissance unit by assisting in identification of enemy reconnaissance and main body elements and by providing early warning forward of the reconnaissance unit. In addition to acquiring enemy forces, UASs can play a critical role in providing security through the depth of the screen by observing dead space between ground observation posts. They can also support the reconnaissance unit during area security missions by screening or conducting reconnaissance.

Reconnaissance/Target Handover

3-43. When a UAS makes contact, particularly during reconnaissance operations, the operator hands over the contact to ground or attack reconnaissance units as quickly as possible. Rapid handover allows the UAS to avoid enemy air defense weapons and also helps to maintain the tempo of the operation. During the handover, the UAS assists in providing direction to the ground or attack reconnaissance unit charged with establishing contact with or engaging the enemy. It maintains contact with the enemy until the units are in position and have established sensor or visual contact.

3-44. The first action in the handover process is a report (such as, spot report or situation report) from the UAS operator to the ground or attack reconnaissance unit. Next, the UAS reconnoiters the area for secure positions for the unit, such as hide, overwatch, observation posts or BPs, and likely mounted and dismounted routes into the area. The ground or attack reconnaissance unit moves to initial hide positions along the route selected by the leader based on UAS-collected information. The ground or attack reconnaissance unit then moves to establish sensor or visual contact with the enemy. Once this contact is established, the ground or attack reconnaissance unit sends a report to the UAS operator. When the UAS operator confirms that the ground or attack unit can observe enemy elements and has a clear picture of the situation, handover is complete. The UAS can then be dedicated to another mission or, in the case of target handover to attack reconnaissance units, may be utilized for BDA and reattack if necessary.

This page intentionally left blank.

Chapter 4

Landing Plan

The landing plan supports the ground tactical plan. It provides a sequence for arrival of units into the AO, ensuring that all assigned units arrive at designated locations and times prepared to execute the ground tactical plan. General considerations for developing the landing plan follow.

SECTION I - LANDING ZONE SELECTION

4-1. Landing zones are usually selected by the AATFC or his S-3 based on technical advice from the AMC or the AVN LNO. Criteria for selecting LZs include the following:

- **Location.** In general, two options are viable when selecting LZs: land on the objective or land away from the objective. The selection of either option is METT-TC dependent.
- **Capacity.** Size determines how much combat power can be inserted at one time and the need for additional LZs or time separation between serials.
- **Types of loads.** Some external loads may dictate the minimum size required for an LZ (such as, CH-47 sling loading a vehicle).
- **Elevation.** The altitude of potential LZs may not be supportable due to operating restrictions of certain aircraft.
- **Alternates.** An alternate LZ should be planned for each primary LZ to ensure flexibility to support the mission.
- **Enemy composition, disposition, and capabilities.** Landing zone considerations include enemy force concentrations and weapons systems and their capability to react to an AATF landing nearby.
- **Cover and concealment.** Landing zones are selected to deny enemy observation and acquisition of friendly ground and air elements while they are en route to, from, or in the LZ.
- **Obstacles.** If possible, the AATF should land on the enemy side of obstacles when attacking to negate their effectiveness. The AATF should consider using obstacles to protect LZs from the enemy at other times. Landing zones should be generally free of obstacles.
- **Identification from the air.** If possible, LZs should be easily identifiable from the air or marked by friendly reconnaissance units that have reconnoitered the LZ.
- **Approach and departure routes.** If possible, approach and departure air routes should avoid continued unnecessary exposure of aircraft to the enemy.
- **Weather.** Reduced visibility or strong winds may preclude or limit the use of primary or alternate LZs.

LOCATION OF LANDING ZONES

4-2. The AATFC considers landing away from the objective when the—

- Air assault task force is assigned an enemy-oriented mission.
- Commander has incomplete or unknown intelligence on the enemy.
- Commander has incomplete information on terrain (especially LZs), weather is not favorable, or no suitable LZs are available near the objective.
- Shaping operations have not set conditions for air assault execution or conditions cannot be verified.
- Time is available upon landing in the LZ to develop the situation.
- Civilian population is unknown or hostile to U.S. presence in the AO.

4-3.   The AATFC considers landing on or near the objective when the—
- Air assault task force is assigned a terrain-oriented mission.
- Commander has accurate up-to-date intelligence on the enemy.
- Commander has accurate intelligence on terrain (especially LZs), weather is favorable, and suitable LZs are available on or near the objective.
- Shaping operations have set conditions for air assault execution.
- Time in which to accomplish the overall mission is limited.
- Civilian population is known to be supportive of U.S. presence in the AO.

NUMBER OF LANDING ZONES

4-4.   The AATFC decides whether to use a single LZ or multiple LZs. A large number of LZs for an air assault increases the tactical risk and complexity of the operation as well as the difficulty of setting conditions at each LZ prior to landing. Whether away from or on the objective, the AATFC should plan for one primary LZ and one alternate LZ per maneuver unit. He should plan for more than one primary and one alternate LZ per maneuver unit only after careful analysis of the mission variables to determine if sufficient units are available to conduct shaping operations at each LZ.

4-5.   Using a single LZ—
- Requires less planning and rehearsal time.
- Allows concentration of combat power in one location.
- Facilitates control of the operation.
- Concentrates supporting fires in and around the LZ. Firepower is diffused if more than one LZ preparation is required.
- Requires fewer attack helicopters for security.
- Provides better security for subsequent lifts.
- Reduces the number of air routes in the objective area, making it more difficult for the enemy to detect the air assault operation.
- Centralizes any required resupply operations.

4-6.   Using multiple LZs—
- Avoids grouping units in one location, which creates a lucrative target for enemy mortars, artillery, and close air support.
- Allows rapid dispersal of ground elements to accomplish tasks in separate areas.
- Reduces the enemy's ability to detect and react to the initial lift.
- Forces the enemy to fight in more than one direction.
- Reduces the possibility of troop congestion in one LZ.
- Eliminates aircraft congestion on one LZ.
- Makes it difficult for the enemy to determine the size of the air assault force and the exact location of supporting weapons.

SECTION II - LANDING ZONE UPDATES

4-7.   Just prior to the start of the air movement and about 2 minutes out from the RP, the attack aviation aircraft provide an LZ update to the AATF, informing the AATFC, GTC, and AMC of the status of enemy activity on the LZ. The requirement for an LZ update is METT-TC dependent and based on the need to preserve surprise on the objective. The manner in which the LZ update is conducted should not divulge the exact location of the LZ.

4-8.   The LZ is considered *cold* if no enemy activity is observed. If the LZ is cold, the air assault is executed as planned. The LZ is considered *hot* if enemy activity is occurring on or near the LZ. If the LZ is hot, the attack aviation aircraft provide a situation report consisting of enemy activity, their actions toward the enemy, a recommendation of how to eliminate or neutralize enemy activity on the LZ to achieve a cold status, and a recommendation for using the alternate LZ. Based on the recommendation of the attack aviation element, the AATFC decides whether to use an alternate LZ. As part of the mission analysis and rehearsal process, aircrews rehearse and execute the air movement using an alternate LZ.

4-9.   When available, fixed-wing aircraft can be used to provide an LZ update or to eliminate enemy activity. As long as lift aircraft or attack aviation aircraft possess the proper communication capabilities, fixed-wing aircraft can relay the update directly to the AATFC. If these capabilities are not present, fixed-wing aircraft may relay the update to a CP that then relays the update to the AATFC. The plan must account for time needed to relay the update to all parties.

4-10. Unmanned aircraft systems can also be employed to monitor and relay the updated status of the LZ and surrounding area during the air movement phase. This early information gives the AATFC more time to adjust plans if required. Unmanned aircraft systems that fly at higher altitudes may observe with negligible risk of revealing LZ or objective locations.

SECTION III - HOT LANDING ZONE PROCEDURES

4-11. Sometimes the presence of enemy activity is unknown or unclear until the first aircraft lands in the LZ. A unit should develop and rehearse its plan for reacting to enemy contact in that situation.

4-12. The enemy may employ one or a combination of the following actions to oppose landing operations:
- Conduct a near ambush.
- Conduct a far ambush.
- Deliver indirect fires by mortars, artillery, or rockets directed by an observer that can see the LZ.
- Emplace obstacles, such as antipersonnel mines, booby traps, or other barriers.

4-13. The AATFC considers five options in response to a hot LZ:
- Fight through the contact.
- Divert to the alternate LZ.
- Abort remaining serials.
- Slow airspeeds to delay serials.
- Racetrack serials. All serials orbit at their current position. Once the enemy has been neutralized or destroyed on the LZ, the air assault resumes in the order outlined in the air movement table. Racetracking is considered a high risk option. The AMC determines whether enough fuel, spacing, and time is available between serials to conduct this option and advises the AATFC accordingly.

4-14. The AATFC makes the final decision on all options involving a hot LZ, and the AMC and GTC execute. Whether landing away from or on the objective, it is important that primary and alternate LZs are mutually supporting to allow the AATFC to shift the main effort if necessary.

REACTION TO ENEMY CONTACT AWAY FROM THE OBJECTIVE

4-15.   When landing away from the objective, ground units can more readily divert to an alternate LZ. In doing so, the main effort of the decisive operation may be shifted to the unit landing at the alternate LZ, and the unit at the hot LZ may be extracted or continue to fight through the enemy contact. If the alternate LZ is hot as well, the AATFC should choose which unit to designate as the main effort to accomplish the decisive operation.

4-16.   A unit that encounters a near ambush, unless extremely successful in counteracting that ambush, is usually extracted, reorganized, and reinserted into an alternate LZ to continue the mission. A unit that encounters a far ambush, hostile indirect fires, or obstacles usually continues its mission.

REACTION TO ENEMY CONTACT ON THE OBJECTIVE

4-17.   When landing on the objective, units normally react to contact and fight through. Because the LZ is on the objective, fighting for control of the hot LZ is critical to mission accomplishment and continuing the assault is the priority. The unit on the hot LZ may be directed to fix the enemy, while the main effort is shifted to the unit that lands at an alternate LZ and fights through to the objective.

4-18. If the alternate LZ is hot as well, the AATFC should choose which unit to designate as the main effort to accomplish the decisive operation. Given the overall mission, breaking contact or extraction is not likely for units caught on a hot LZ. In cases other than a near ambush, units normally fight through enemy contact and continue the mission without diverting serials to an alternate LZ.

SECTION IV – PREPARATORY AND SUPPORTING FIRES

4-19. Preparatory fires are planned for each LZ so they can be executed if needed. However, it is desirable to make the initial assault without preparatory fires in order to achieve tactical surprise. Planned fires for air assault operations should be intense and short but with a high volume of fire to maximize the surprise and shock effect.

4-20. When developing FS plans, consider—

- **Deception.** False preparations are fired into areas other than the objective or LZ area to deceive enemy forces.
- **Duration of preparatory fires.** A preparation of long duration may reduce the possibility of surprise. The preparatory fires should begin as the first aircraft of the first lift crosses the RP and end just before the first aircraft lands.
- **Availability of fire support assets.** The FSO coordinates with the artillery unit to arrange the preparation of units that can fire. In some cases, where an air assault is executed across extended distances, preparatory fires by close air support or attack helicopters may be the only viable alternative.
- **High-value targets.** A known or suspected enemy force in the landing area, regardless of size, warrants an LZ preparation.
- **Effects of ordnances on the LZ.** Some ordnances used in preparatory fires (such as artillery, bombs, or infrared illumination) may be undesirable since they can cause craters, downed trees, fires, and LZ obscuration.
- **Scheduling fires.** Fires are scheduled to be lifted or shifted to coincide with the arrival times of aircraft formations.
- **Positive control measures.** Control measures must be established for lifting or shifting fires.

SECTION V – LANDING AND EXITING THE AIRCRAFT

4-21. Aircraft formations on the LZ should facilitate a rapid exit from the aircraft, an orderly departure off the LZ, and an organized deployment for the assault. The number and type of aircraft and the configuration and size of the LZ may dictate the formation. If contact is expected in the LZ, elements must land ready to fight and maneuver in all directions. (See FM 3-04.113 for details on aircraft landing formations.)

4-22. An LZ formation may not have standardized distances between aircraft due to the size or terrain on the LZ. The goal in landing aircraft successfully is to select a safe landing area as close to cover and concealment as possible to reduce troop exposure. If possible, the aircraft formation on the PZ is the same as the LZ. This provides Soldiers and leaders a preview of the LZ landing formation and gives them an idea of their location upon landing in relation to other elements.

4-23. Normally, the lead elements lifted into the LZ are responsible for clearing the LZ to support follow-on lifts. This can be accomplished using a number of techniques, which are entirely METT-TC dependent. The most common technique for clearing the LZ is to assign assault objectives, which requires subordinate units to move through an assigned area to clear enemy forces prior to reaching their final objective.

EXITING THE AIRCRAFT

4-24. The two techniques for exiting a UH-60 aircraft are the one-side off-load and the two-side off-load. Soldiers exiting a CH-47 do so from the rear ramp. In each technique, Soldiers must be careful to avoid the main and tail rotors of the aircraft they are exiting and the rotors of other aircraft in their serial. The separation between serials and the number of serials that can fit into the LZ at one time are critical planning considerations when determining the aircraft exiting technique.

ONE-SIDE OFF-LOAD

4-25. In this technique, Soldiers exit from either the right or left side of the aircraft (Figure 4-1). Soldiers exiting the aircraft should step outward and take up a prone position, forming 180-degree security on that side of the aircraft yet remaining under the main rotor system and outside the landing gear of the aircraft. Soldiers should remain in the prone position until the aircraft lifts off before departing the LZ. The chalk leader directs his chalk to move to the nearest covered and concealed position in accordance with the landing plan or standing operating procedures.

4-26. A unit plans to execute a one-side off-load on the side away from known or potential enemy positions but may be forced to exit the aircraft on the opposite side due to the enemy or other METT-TC considerations once the aircraft has landed.

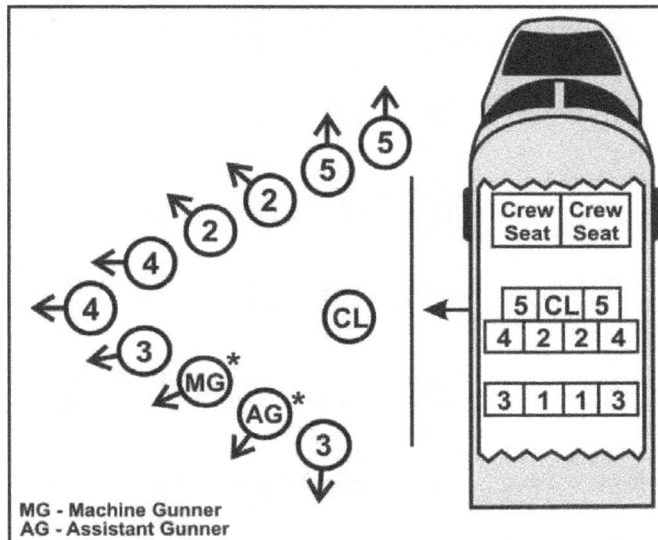

Figure 4-1. One-side off-load (UH-60)

Advantages

4-27. The one-side off-load simplifies C2 and the establishment of zones of responsibility on the LZ. It allows the door gunners on the opposite side of the aircraft to engage enemy positions during off-loading (Figure 4-2) and allows the door gunners of follow-on serials to engage enemy on the far side of the LZ.

Disadvantages

4-28. The one-side off-load is the slowest of the off-loading techniques. The Soldiers and aircraft are exposed for a longer amount of time while exiting the aircraft, making them vulnerable to direct and indirect fire.

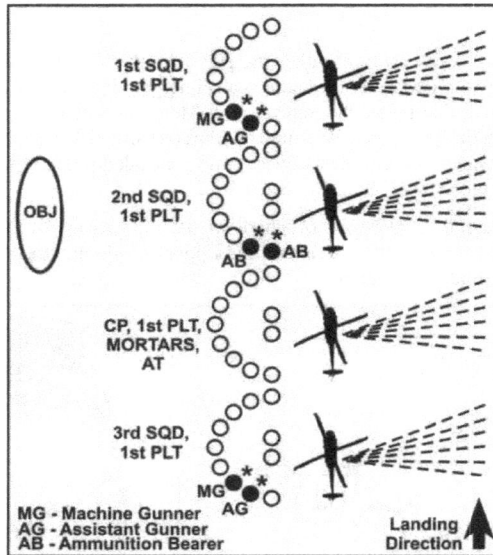

Figure 4-2. One-side off-load (enemy on right side)

TWO-SIDE OFF-LOAD

4-29. In this technique, Soldiers exit from both sides of the aircraft (Figure 4-3). Soldiers exiting the aircraft should step outward and take up a prone position, forming 180-degree security on that side of the aircraft yet remaining under the main rotor system and outside the landing gear of the aircraft. Soldiers should remain in the prone position until the aircraft lifts off before departing the LZ. The squad leader directs his squad to move directly to the nearest covered and concealed position in accordance with the landing plan or standing operating procedures.

4-30. Cross-load options allow for pure unit integrity of chalks (Figure 4-4) or mixed loads to support moving to opposite sides of a large PZ (Figure 4-5). Cross-load planning considerations support the C2 initially required on the LZ and follow-on lifts into the LZ.

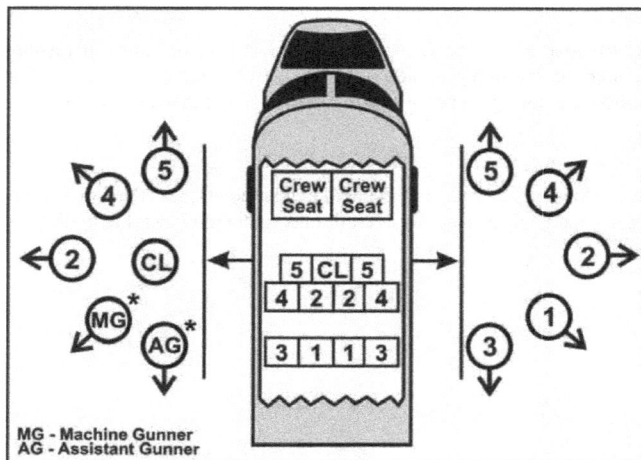

Figure 4-3. Two-side off-load (UH-60)

Advantages

4-31. The two-sided off-load is the quickest technique for exiting the aircraft. It simplifies control and the establishment of zones of responsibility on the LZ.

Disadvantages

4-32. The two-sided off-load has the slowest movement time off the LZ of all off-loading techniques, which exposes Soldiers longer to enemy direct and indirect fire. This technique also masks both door gunner fires while Soldiers exit the aircraft, which increases vulnerability to enemy direct fire.

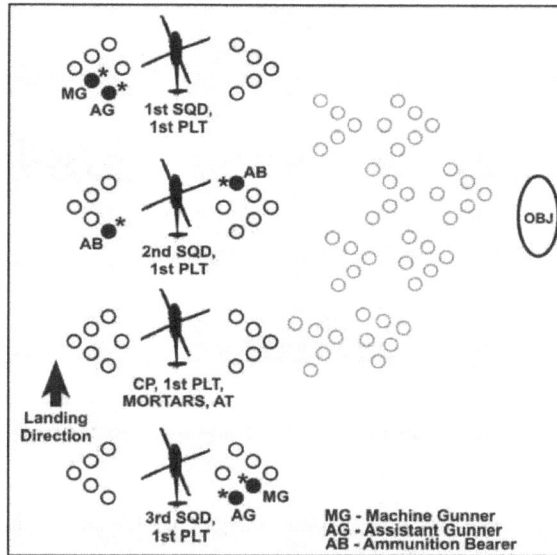

Figure 4-4. Two-side off-load (squads in same chalk)

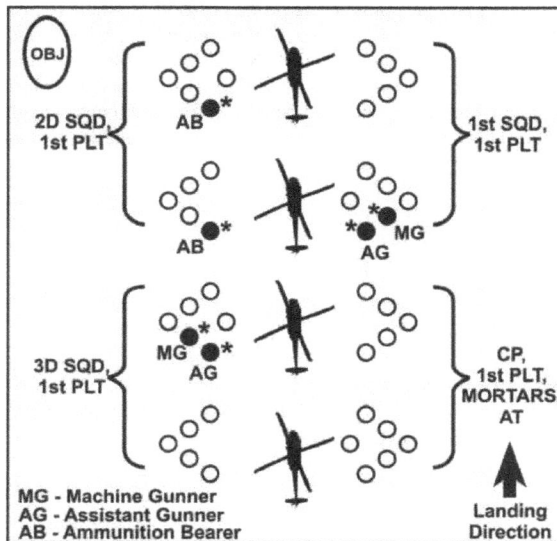

Figure 4-5. Two-side off-load (chalks cross-loaded)

REAR RAMP OFF-LOAD

4-33. In this technique, Soldiers exit from the rear ramp of a CH-47 or CH-47 variant aircraft. Soldiers move out from the aircraft and drop to a prone fighting position, establishing 360-degree security until the aircraft lifts to depart the LZ (Figure 4-6). Once the aircraft departs the LZ, the unit may execute a one-side or two-side LZ rush in accordance with the landing plan or standing operating procedures.

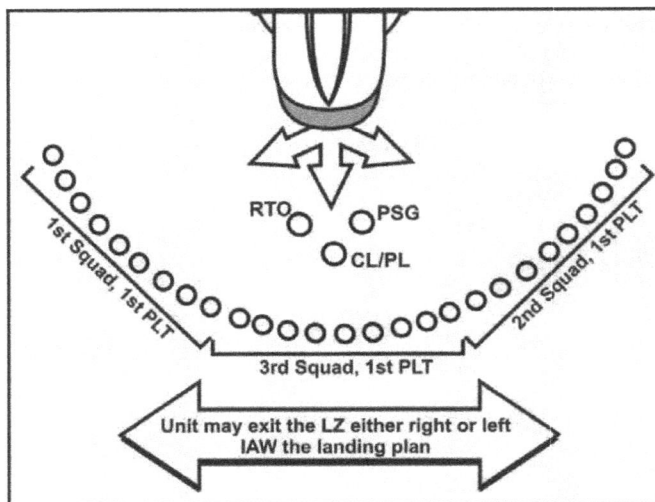

Figure 4-6. Example rear ramp off-load and landing zone exit (CH-47)

EXITING THE LANDING ZONE

4-34. The two techniques for departing the LZ after exiting the aircraft are described below.

ONE-SIDE LANDING ZONE RUSH

4-35. Upon exiting the aircraft and dropping to the prone position, Soldiers recover from the prone position and move immediately with their squad to a covered and concealed position (such as a tree line) in wedge or other formation determined by their squad leader. Squads assemble at designated rally points and then move to assault objectives on the LZ or to objectives off the LZ. This is the preferred method to use when touchdown points are near covered and concealed positions. The unit may plan a one-side LZ rush away from a potential enemy position, allowing the door gunner closest to the enemy position to continue firing while Soldiers exit the other side of the aircraft (Figure 4-7).

Advantages

4-36. A one-side LZ rush—
- Moves the unit off the danger area quickly.
- Facilitates control.
- Maintains momentum and is less vulnerable to indirect fires.
- Simplifies establishing zones of responsibility on the LZ.
- Minimizes aircraft cross-loading plans.
- Allows door gunner of off-loading and follow-on serials to engage enemy on the far side of the LZ.
- Clears the LZ quickly for follow-on lifts.

Disadvantages

4-37. The unit executing a one-side LZ rush is vulnerable to direct fire weapons while moving off the LZ.

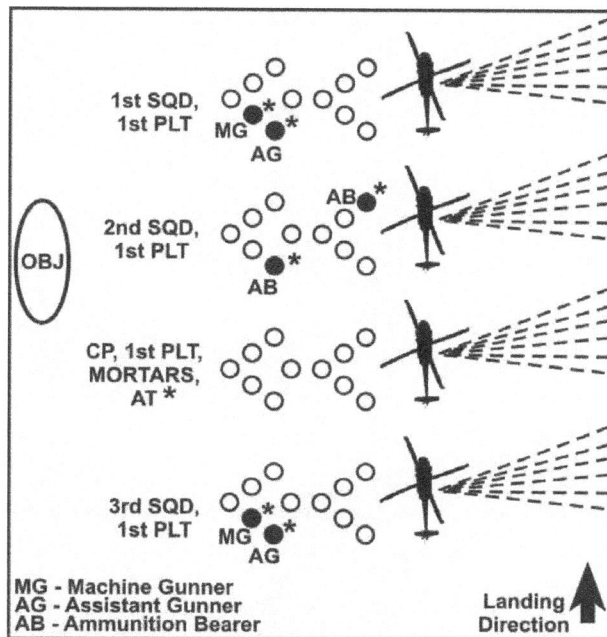

Figure 4-7. One-side landing zone rush

TWO-SIDE LANDING ZONE RUSH

4-38. Aircraft loading options to consider when using a two-side LZ rush are to—
- Split the squad across two chalks, with each fire team exiting the same door (Figure 4-8).
- Keep each chalk as a pure squad, with even-numbered chalks exiting the right door and odd-numbered chalks exiting the left door or vice versa (Figure 4-9).

4-39. Upon exiting the aircraft and dropping to the prone position, Soldiers recover from the prone position and move immediately with their squad to a covered and concealed position in wedge or other formation designated by their squad leader. Squads assemble at designated rally points and then move to assault objectives on the LZ or to objectives off the LZ. The aircraft landing formation can help facilitate the unit in rapidly clearing Soldiers off the LZ.

Advantages

4-40. A two-side LZ rush—
- Moves the unit off the danger area fastest.
- Facilitates clearing and securing of the LZ.
- Facilitates fire control measures on the LZ.
- Maintains momentum and is less vulnerable to indirect fires.
- Establishes zones of responsibility on the LZ.
- Clears the LZ quickly for follow-on lifts.

Disadvantages

4-41. A two-side LZ rush is more difficult to plan and control due to its complex aircraft cross-loading plan. It also masks fires of both door gunners while departing the LZ, which increases vulnerability to direct fire while moving off the LZ.

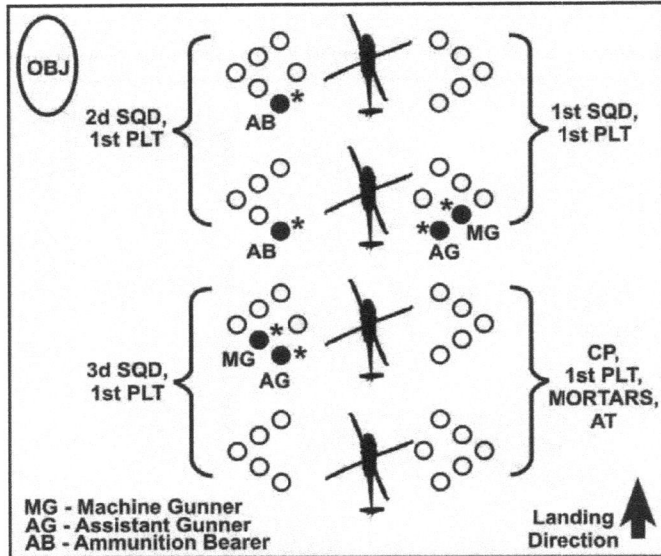

Figure 4-8. Two-side landing zone rush (chalks cross-loaded)

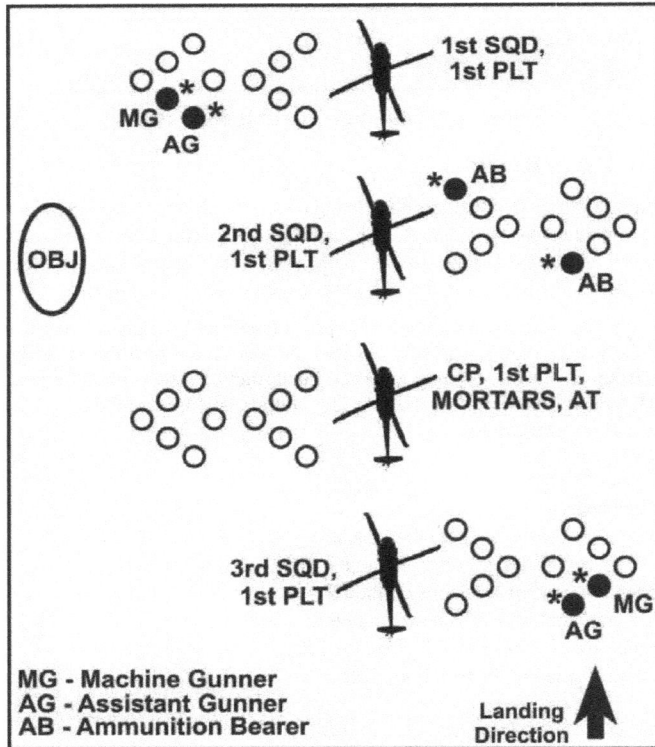

Figure 4-9. Two-side landing zone rush (squads in same chalk)

Chapter 5

Air Movement Plan

The air movement plan is largely based on the ground tactical plan and landing plan. It begins when the assault or lift helicopters cross the start point (SP) and ends when they cross the RP. The air movement plan specifies the schedule and provides instructions for air movement of Soldiers, equipment, and supplies from the PZ to the LZ. The air movement plan considers the impact of airspace restrictions. It also provides coordinating instructions regarding air routes, aircraft speeds, altitudes, formations, and the planned use of attack helicopters.

SECTION I – DEVELOPMENT CONSIDERATIONS

5-1.   The air movement plan is developed by the AATF and supporting aviation unit staffs in coordination with technical assistance and recommendations from the BAE, AMC, and the AVN LNO. The aviation unit conducts all air mission planning using the Aviation Mission Planning System (AMPS). This allows the aviation unit to plan digitally, allowing rapid distribution of digital products among units within the AATF. However, the AATFC approves the final plan. The end result of air movement planning is the completion of the air movement table, which specifies the AATF movement from the PZ to the LZ.

5-2.   Important considerations when developing the air movement plan are described below.

AIR ROUTES

5-3.   Components of an air route are the—
- Start point.
- Release point.
- Air control points.
- Flight path between the SP and RP.

5-4.   The air route starts at the SP and ends at the RP. The location of SPs and RPs are usually 3 to 5 kilometers from the PZs and LZs respectively to allow adequate flying time for execution of the flight's en route procedures. The distance from the PZ to the SP allows the aircraft to achieve the desired airspeed, altitude, and formation after liftoff. The distance from the RP to the LZ allows the flight leader to reconfigure the formation and execute a tactical formation landing. The designated locations of the SPs and RPs should—
- Profit from favorable weather conditions.
- Avoid obstacles and known enemy positions.
- Facilitate takeoff and landing into the wind by the best air route.

5-5.   Air control points designate each point where the air route changes direction. They include readily identifiable topographic features or points marked by electronic navigational aids. A route may have as many air control points as necessary to control the air movement. The SPs and RPs are also air control points.

5-6.   Once identified, air routes are designated for use by each unit. When large groups of aircraft are employed, dispersion is achieved by using multiple routes. However, with large serials, it is often necessary to use fewer routes or even a single route to concentrate available supporting fires. Also, the number of alternate and return routes may be limited.

5-7.   Regardless of direction or location, certain criteria apply. All characteristics are seldom present in any one situation, but all should be considered. Give careful consideration to the terrain and enemy forces. Air routes should assist in navigation (day or night) and avoid turns in excess of 60 degrees to facilitate control of the aircraft formation when formation flying is required or if sling loads are involved.

5-8. When selecting routes, consider the following factors:

- **Interference with ground action.** Overflying ground elements may interfere with their supporting fire. Clear air routes of the gun-target line when possible. Avoid overflight of built-up areas.
- **Support of landing plan.** To reduce vulnerability of the air assault force, air routes facilitate rapid approach, landing, and departure from selected LZs.
- **Enemy ground and air capabilities.** Air routes maximize use of terrain, cover, and concealment to minimize exposure to enemy observation, target acquisition, and direct fire.
- **Available fire support.** Air routes allow FS from all available resources. Avoid masking friendly fires, particularly supporting fires.
- **Available air cover.** Air routes are selected to provide air cover for friendly forces en route.
- **Weather conditions.** Prevailing weather during the air assault operation significantly affects the selection of air routes.
- **Terrain.** Air routes use terrain to maximum the advantage of and reduce vulnerability of the aircraft formations, providing cover by placing terrain mass and vegetation between the enemy and the aircraft.
- **Distance from PZ to LZ.** Air routes should be as short as is tactically feasible in accordance with mission variables to reduce flying time.

5-9. Maps or overlays containing air route information are prepared at aviation unit headquarters and disseminated to subordinate and support units. Air routes and corridors are designated by a letter, number, or word. (See Figure 5-1.)

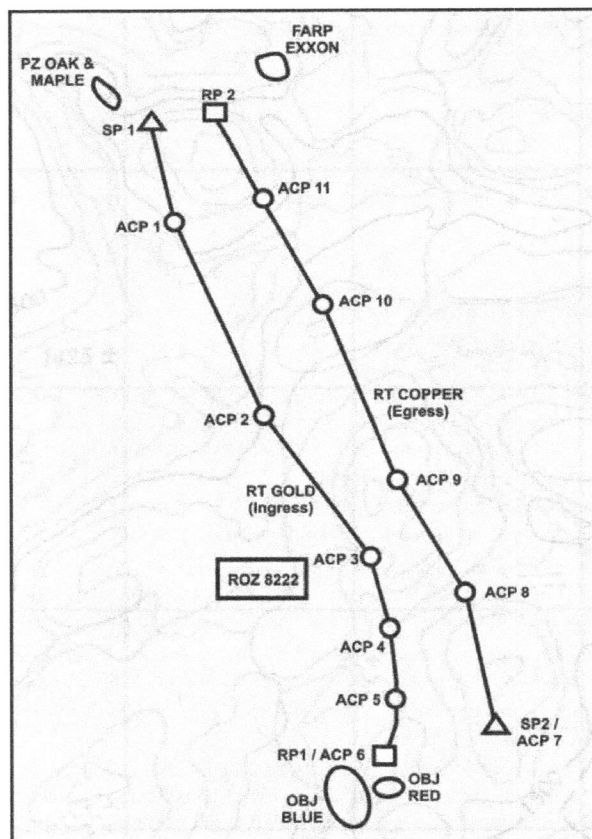

Figure 5-1. Example air route overlay

EN ROUTE FORMATIONS

5-10. Many factors dictate the flight's formation, such as terrain, enemy situation, visibility, weather, altitude, speed, type of aircraft mix, and the degree of control required. The AMC or flight leader selects the en route and landing formation based on the mission variables. Ideally, the aircraft land in the formation specified by the air movement table.

TERRAIN FLIGHT MODES

5-11. A specific en route flight altitude is not designated and is usually below the coordinating altitude. Factors affecting flight altitude include enemy, terrain, navigation, weather, flight distance, need for surprise, and pilot fatigue. Pilots may use one or a combination of all three terrain flight modes as dictated by the mission variables:

- **Nap-of-the-earth flight** is conducted at varying airspeeds as close to the earth's surface as vegetation and obstacles permit. It is a weaving flight path that remains oriented along the general axis of movement and takes advantage of terrain masking. This is a general flight mode and may likely be in close proximity to the enemy.
- **Contour flight** is conducted at low altitudes, conforming to the earth's contours. It is characterized by relatively constant airspeeds and varying altitudes as dictated by terrain and obstacles.
- **Low-level flight** is conducted at constant altitudes and airspeed dictated by threat avoidance. Its intent is to facilitate speed and ease of movement while minimizing detection. This mode of flight is used when there is a low threat level.

FIRES

5-12. Fires along the air route are planned to suppress known or suspected enemy positions. These fires should be intense and of short duration. Utilize multiple target engagement techniques as necessary. On-call fires are planned along the air route to ensure rapid target engagement if necessary.

5-13. Fire plans cover the PZs, air routes, and LZs. FS plans include SEAD systems and obscuration to protect formations from enemy detection. This requires aggressive fire planning by the FSO and direct coordination with field artillery and mortar fire direction centers and other FS elements.

5-14. All available FS is used to suppress or destroy enemy weapons, including tactical air, artillery, and attack helicopters. Support may consist of concealment or other countermeasures for suppressing or confusing enemy air defense systems. During night operations, the use of illumination fire requires detailed planning. Illumination can interfere with night vision goggles, causing unsafe conditions.

SUPPRESSION OF ENEMY AIR DEFENSES

5-15. In executing air movement, the AMC integrates air routes based on PZ and LZ locations, avoiding known or suspected enemy air defense positions. The AATF FSO is responsible for planning, synchronizing, and executing lethal and nonlethal suppressive fires on known or suspected enemy air defense positions that are unavoidable. Lethal and nonlethal assets available to conduct SEAD missions include—

- Mortars and cannon, rocket, and missile artillery.
- Fixed-wing assets, including UASs.
- Naval gunfire.
- Attack reconnaissance helicopters.
- Radar suppression and jamming (lethal and nonlethal).
- Communications suppression and jamming (lethal and nonlethal).
- Other electronic warfare and electronic attack assets.

5-16. The term Joint SEAD encompasses all SEAD activities provided by components of a joint force in support of one another. When operating as a component of a joint force, different assets and unique planning requirements may exist. (See JP 3-01 for details.) Joint SEAD includes all SEAD categories and additional classifications to include—

- **Operational area system suppression** consists of operations within an operational area against specific enemy air defense systems to degrade or destroy their effectiveness. It targets high-payoff air defense systems whose degradation most greatly impacts the enemy's total system.
- **Opportune suppression** is a continuous operation involving immediate attack of air defense targets of opportunity. It is normally unplanned suppression and includes aircrew self-defense and attacks against targets of opportunity.
- **Localized suppression** can occur throughout the area of responsibility or joint operations area and can be conducted by all components. However, it is limited in time and geographical areas associated with specific ground targets.
- **Corridor suppression** is planned joint SEAD focused on creating an air defense artillery suppressed corridor to maneuver aircraft. It may be requested by any component to the joint force through normal channels. Missions that normally require this suppression are air missions supporting tactical airlift or combat operations, search and rescue operations, and operations in support of special operations forces.

PLANNING

5-17. The ground maneuver, aviation units, AATF operations officers, AATF intelligence officers, and electronic warfare officer participate in SEAD planning. SEAD planning is conducted as part of the MDMP and targeting process. Critical factors to consider in mission analysis are—

- Ingress and egress air routes and locations of air control points.
- En route airspeed.
- Time, distance, and heading information for primary and alternate air routes.
- Expected SP crossing time on ingress and egress.
- Enemy air defense artillery locations within the AO.
- Locations, frequencies, and call signs of friendly artillery.
- Available assets to deliver SEAD fires.

5-18. When determining enemy air defense capabilities, mission planners—

- Plot the location of all known enemy air defense artillery systems on a map.
- Draw a circle (threat ring) around each air defense artillery system with a radius equal to the maximum engagement range. Depending on the threat system and its means of target acquisition (optical, infrared, and radar) and fire control, the size of the threat ring may change during hours of limited visibility. Terrain that blocks electronic or visual lines of sight may reduce the radius of a threat ring.
- Use AMPS, Falcon View, or other automated systems to reduce workload and ensure accuracy.
- Plot the primary and alternate air routes and all LZs on the map. Air routes and LZs should avoid threat rings whenever possible.

5-19. Plan SEAD fires to engage the two types of targets described below.

Planned Targets

5-20. Two types of planned targets are—

- **Scheduled targets** that are prosecuted at a specified time.
- **On-call targets** that have planned actions and are triggered when detected or located.

5-21. Deception SEAD may be fired into an area to deceive the enemy or cause him to reposition his air defense weapons away from where actual operations take place. Electronic attack of enemy air defense radars and C2 systems should be considered, particularly when enemy air defense artillery assets are in civilian populated areas.

5-22. Ensure provisions exist for immediate on-call fires in the SEAD plan. The FSO may establish a quick-fire net for this purpose. A quick-fire net provides a direct link between an observer and weapon system (normally field artillery). Observers are ordered based on their priority of fire. Conduct a FS rehearsal with the supporting unit. Brief and rehearse with all participants during the combined arms rehearsal.

Targets of Opportunity

5-23. SEAD is conducted against air defense artillery targets of opportunity and should reflect priorities established on the high-payoff target list and attack guidance matrix. Delivery systems and quick-fire nets are critical to engaging targets of opportunity.

EMPLOYMENT

5-24. SEAD fires should be planned against any enemy air defense artillery system that threatens the air assault force. A period of focused immediate SEAD is normally planned at each LZ prior to the arrival of the AATF. If possible, plan deception SEAD to further mitigate tactical risk.

5-25. Scheduled SEAD missions are planned against threat systems along the ingress and egress route of flight. The start time for each SEAD mission may be calculated if the assault aircraft's en route airspeed and SP time on the air route are known. These calculations may be made manually or with AMPS or similar planning systems.

5-26. Factors that determine the duration of each SEAD mission include aircraft speed and the range of each enemy air defense artillery system (size of the threat ring). This information may be used with planning software to determine how long to suppress each air defense artillery system along the air route. Calculations may be made manually or estimated. A good planning estimate is that the air assault will travel 3 kilometers in 1 minute.

5-27. Position units to support as much of the AO as possible. To ensure synchronization, organize all planned fires into an SEAD schedule or add them to the execution matrix. Assess the effectiveness of the SEAD plan during war gaming.

AIR ASSAULT SECURITY

5-28. Air assault security is conducted throughout the air movement phase. Air assault security is not necessarily just an escort mission. The air assault security process can be conducted sequentially, simultaneously, or over a period of 24 to 72 hours before the start of the air assault mission. This process is determined early in the mission analysis phase and is a direct result of the AATFCs initial guidance and key tasks.

5-29. Unmanned aircraft systems should observe the air routes and LZs beginning well before launch to provide early warning to the AATFC. Normally, just before the launch of the air movement phase, attack reconnaissance units fly along the route to conduct an air assault security mission. This mission is much like a movement to contact. Usually, one to two attack reconnaissance companies conduct the mission just before the assault aircraft launch for the air movement. This allows the attack reconnaissance units opportunity to conduct a relief on station with elements that may already be on station providing reconnaissance.

5-30. The air assault security force generally makes the final LZ update call as the assault forces are en route to the LZ. Prior to assault forces landing on the LZ, air assault security forces may be directed to shift to an LZ overwatch mission, ensuring they do not conflict with the air routes entering or exiting the LZ. As the assault forces land on the LZ, air assault security forces may be directed to move forward to the next phase line to conduct a screening mission or to occupy a battle position.

5-31. Attack reconnaissance units maintain the flexibility to execute on-call CCAs as needed. Air assault security units must maintain communications with the fires elements for immediate suppression missions as necessary. (See FM 3-04.126 for details.)

COMMAND AND CONTROL PROCEDURES

5-32. In executing the air movement, the AMC takes OPCON of all Army aviation forces. The AMC controls all—

- Timing for deconfliction.
- En route fires.
- Initiation and shifting of LZ preparatory fires.

5-33. Once the air assault force has cleared the LZ and moved to its rally point, the tactical commander on the ground assumes C2 of the element and continues his assigned mission. Command and control procedures should allow continued execution despite loss of radio communications. If the AMC and lift flight leaders have air movement tables or the execution checklist in their possession, they can continue the mission without radio communications.

SECTION II – AIR MOVEMENT TABLE

5-34. The air movement table—

- Contains aircraft allocations.
- Designates number and type of aircraft in each serial.
- Specifies departure point; route to and from loading area; and loading, liftoff, and landing times.
- Includes the refuel schedule for all lifts if required.

5-35. The AATF staff and aviation unit staff prepare jointly the air movement table in detail, since it serves as the primary air movement document. The AATF S-3 air and AVN LNO begin work on this document right after the IPC. This gives them an idea early in the planning process of any challenges involved in moving units to the LZ. The table ensures that all personnel, equipment, and supplies are accounted for in the movement and that each aircraft is fully loaded, correctly positioned in the flight, and directed to the right LZ. (See Chapter 2 for an example of a completed air movement table.)

Chapter 6

Loading and Staging Plans

The activities that take place in or near the PZ are commonly referred to as PZ operations. These activities include both the loading and staging plan. Like the previous steps in the air assault planning process, these plans support and are based on the steps before them.

Pickup zone operations are a collaborative effort between the supported unit (maneuver forces that compose the assault force) and the supporting aviation unit. The assault force is organized on the PZ. Every serial and lift is a self-contained element that must understand what it does upon landing at either the primary or alternate LZ and later in executing the ground tactical plan.

Planning for insertion and extraction follows the same process and requires the same forethought and attention to detail. Insertion and extraction plans are developed during the air assault planning process and coordinated with all supporting units at the initial planning conference or AMCM. Both insertion and extraction loading and staging plans should be rehearsed at the air assault task force rehearsal, aviation rehearsal, and assault force rehearsals.

SECTION I – LOADING PLAN

6-1. The loading plan ensures that Soldiers, equipment, and supplies are loaded on the correct aircraft and moved from the PZ to the LZ in the priority order designated by the AATFC. The air movement table is the planning document that details how to execute this. At the company level and below, leaders use an air loading table to document how the loading plan is executed. The basic information found in the air loading table is also found in the air movement table. (See Chapter 2 for details on air movement tables.)

6-2. Considerations for developing a loading plan are described below.

PICKUP ZONE SELECTION

6-3. Identifying PZs is the first step in developing a loading plan. The goal of PZ identification is to locate suitable areas to accommodate the lift aircraft. Primary and alternate PZs are identified at the same time.

6-4. Establishing and running a PZ to standard is the first step in executing a successful air assault. The number of PZs selected depends on the number and type of aircraft and loads required to complete the mission. The mission may require the designation of both a light PZ (UH-60) and a heavy PZ (CH-47). Based on his evaluation of his unit's level of training, the AMC may adjust the specifications for identifying and selecting PZs, such as degree of slope, wind speeds, and distance between aircraft.

6-5. Once available PZs are identified, the AATFC and his S-3 select and assign PZs for each unit to use. Pickup zone selection criteria include—

- **Number.** Multiple PZs avoid concentrating forces in one area.
- **Size**. If possible, each PZ should accommodate all supporting aircraft at once.
- **Proximity to Soldiers.** When possible, the selected PZs should not require extensive ground movement to the PZ by troops.
- **Accessibility.** Each PZ should be accessible to vehicles to move support assets and assault forces.
- **Vulnerability to attack.** Selected PZs should be masked by terrain from enemy observation.

● **Conditions.** Surface conditions of the area (for example, excessive slope; blowing dust, sand, or snow; and manmade or existing obstacles) create potential hazards to PZ operations.

Note. Using PZs located in secure forward operating bases and outposts precludes much of the effort required to identify and select suitable PZs.

PICKUP ZONE ORGANIZATION AND CONTROL

6-6.   Once the AATFC selects the PZs, he designates a PZCO to organize, control, and coordinate PZ operations. The designated PZCO is usually selected based on experience and the size of unit that is conducting the air assault. For example, at BCT level, the BCT executive officer is usually the PZCO. At battalion level, the battalion executive officer or S-3 Air is usually the PZCO. At company level, the company executive officer is usually the PZCO.

6-7.   Once designated, the PZCO is responsible for the overall success of all PZ activities, to include—

● Forming a control party to establish control over the PZ by clearing the PZ and establishing PZ security. The PZ control party consists of PZ control teams and support personnel from subordinate units, typically including a PZCO, a PZ noncommissioned officer in charge, and—

■ **Chalk guides** who guide the aircraft loads (Soldiers, vehicles, and equipment) from the chalk check-in point to their respective staging areas on the PZ once they have been inspected and approved for loading by the PZ control party.

■ **Ground crew teams** who provide visual guidance to the aircraft pilots and hook up the vehicles and equipment that are externally loaded (sling loaded) by the aircraft. UH-60 ground crew teams typically consist of one hook-up person, one static probe person, and a signal person. CH-47 hook-up teams typically consist of one hook-up person and one static probe person per sling hook-up point.

■ **Crisis action teams** who are experienced officers or noncommissioned officers who are experts with rigging all types of loads and hook-up procedures for all aircraft.

■ **Security teams** who provide local security for all PZ operations. These teams may also include air defense teams if they are available.

■ **Air traffic control teams** (if available) **who** use radio or directional light signals to provide flight information, expedite traffic, and prevent collisions. Pathfinder teams are also capable of serving as air traffic control teams if required.

■ **Pathfinder teams** (if available) who provide air traffic advisories and navigational aid for fixed- and rotary-wing aircraft. They also perform limited physical improvement and CBRN monitoring and surveying within PZs, if required. Pathfinder availability, the tactical plan, the complexity of the operation, the terrain, and the air assault proficiency of the supported ground unit may dictate pathfinder support.

● Establishing communications on two primary radio frequencies: one to control movement and loading of units and one to control aviation elements (combat aviation net). Alternate frequencies are provided as necessary.

● Planning and initiating FS near PZs in coordination with the AATF FSO to provide all-round protection (from available support) without endangering arrival and departure of Soldiers or aircraft.

● Planning and initiating security to protect the main body as it assembles, moves to the PZ, and is lifted out. Other forces should provide security elements if the PZ is within a friendly area. Security comes from AATF resources if a unit is to be extracted from the objective area.

● Marking the PZ as specified in unit standing operating procedures. Regardless of the type of markers, PZ marking requirements depend on the type and number of aircraft and are based on the minimum acceptable distance between aircraft. At a minimum, mark the PZ to indicate where each aircraft, by type, is to land.

● Clearing the PZ of obstacles.

● Executing the bump plan.

COORDINATION WITH SUPPORTING AVIATION UNIT

6-8. Loading plans are carefully coordinated with the BAO and aviation liaison. Copies of the air movement tables and air loading tables should be distributed to the AVN LNO AATFC, AMC, and PZCO.

6-9. The supporting helicopter unit must ensure that aviation expertise is present on the PZ. The BAO or AVN LNO (or another designated representative) should locate with the PZCO during the PZ selection, setup, and execution phase. The aviation representatives provide guidance on the PZ setup, taking aircraft factors into consideration. For example, the PZ landing direction may change if the wind changes significantly. Additionally, the aviation representatives can offer advice on surface conditions and their effect on helicopter operations.

PREPARATION OF AIR LOADING TABLES

6-10. The air loading table assigns personnel and major items of equipment or supplies to a specific aircraft (chalk) at the company and below level. The air loading table is an accountability tool, a loading manifest, for each aircraft. Figure 6-1 shows an example air loading table.

Line #	Avn Unit	Lifted Unit	Lift	Serial	Chalk	PZ	PZ Arr/ Load Time	T/O Time	SP	RP	LZ	LZ Time	Load		Remarks
													PAX	Sling	
1	2-344	A/1-603 IN	2	1	1-4	Maple	H-2+00:00	H-44:40	H-40:21	H-01:38	Robin	H+02:58	4x11 (44)		
2	2-344	A/1-603 IN	2	2	5-8	Maple	H-2+00:00	H-43:40	H-39:21	H+02:38	Robin	H+03:58	4x11 (44)		
3	2-344	A/1-603 IN	2	3	9-12	Maple	H-2+00:00	H-42:40	H-38:21	H+03:38	Robin	H+04:58	4x11 (44)		
4	2-344	A/1-603 IN, HHC 1-603 IN	2	4	13-16	Maple	H-2+00:00	H-41:40	H-37:21	H+04:38	Robin	H+05:58	4x11 (44)		Chalk 13 is the TAC CP

Figure 6-1. Example air loading table

6-11. When time is limited, the table can be written on a sheet of paper. It should contain a list, prepared by the aircraft chalk leader, of Soldiers (by name) and equipment to be loaded on each chalk. This ensures that information on personnel and equipment onboard is available if an aircraft is lost. The chalk leader gives a copy of the air loading table to the PZ control party upon arriving at the PZ for check-in.

6-12. During preparation of the loading tables, leaders at all levels maintain the—

- **Tactical integrity of units.** Load a complete tactical unit, such as a fire team or squad, on the same aircraft or a platoon in the same serial to ensure integrity as a fighting unit upon landing.
- **Tactical cross-loading.** Plane loads so that key personnel and critical equipment (for example, crew-served weapons) are not loaded on the same aircraft. Thus, if an aircraft is lost to an abort or enemy action, the mission is not seriously hampered.
- **Self-sufficiency of loads.** Ensure that each unit load has everything required (weapons, crew, and ammunition) to be operational upon reaching its destination. Ensure that—
  - The prime mover accompanies every towed item.
  - Crews are loaded with their vehicle or weapon systems.
  - Sufficient personnel are onboard to unload cargo carried.

6-13. Leaders must also determine whether internal or external (sling) loading is the best delivery method for equipment and supplies. Helicopters loaded internally can fly faster and are more maneuverable. Helicopters loaded externally fly slower at higher altitudes and are less maneuverable but can be loaded and unloaded more rapidly than internally-loaded helicopters. The method used depends largely on availability of sling and rigging equipment.

DISPOSITION OF LOADS ON PICKUP ZONE

6-14. Position personnel and equipment on the PZ in accordance with the PZ diagram. Flight crews must understand the loading plan and should be prepared to accept Soldiers and equipment immediately on landing. Pickup zone diagrams depicting the location of chalks and sling loads in the PZ assist flight crews in loading troops and equipment quickly once the aircraft arrive in the PZ. Flight crews should be provided a PZ diagram. Figure 6-2 shows an example PZ diagram.

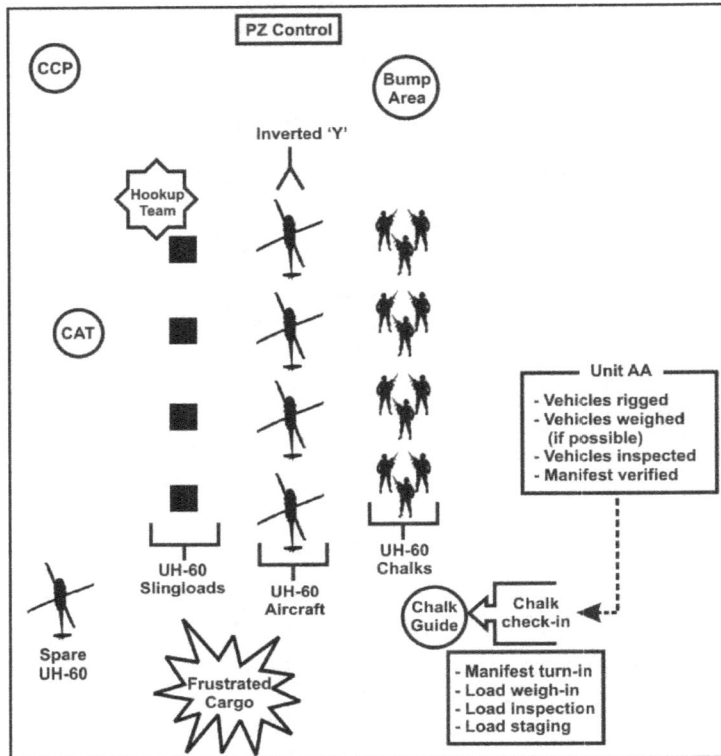

Figure 6-2. Example pickup zone diagram

LIFTS, SERIALS, AND CHALKS

6-15. To maximize OPCON, aviation assets are designated into lifts, serials, and chalks (Figure 6-3).

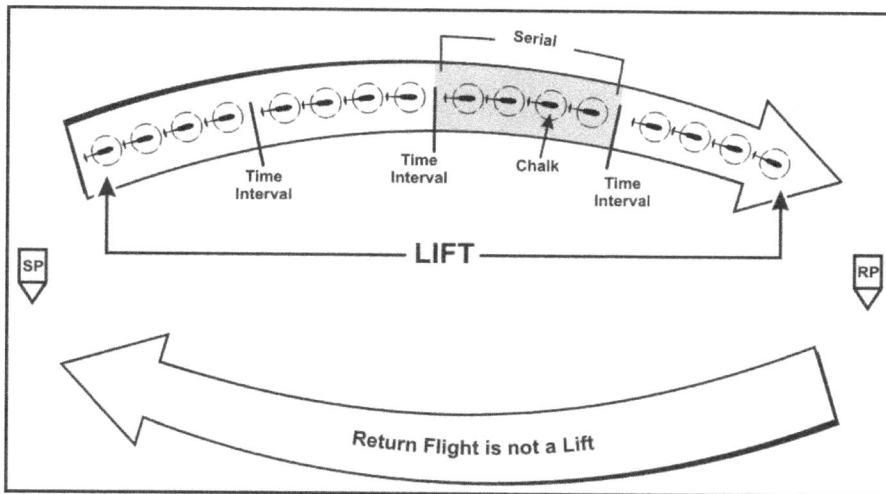

Figure 6-3. Lifts, serials, and chalks

LIFTS

6-16. Each time all aircraft assigned to the mission pick up Soldiers or equipment and set them down on the LZ, a lift is completed. The next lift is completed when all lift aircraft place their next chalk on the LZ and so on with all subsequent lifts.

SERIALS

6-17. A serial is a tactical grouping of two or more aircraft under the control of a serial commander (aviator) and separated from other tactical groupings within the lift by time or space. The use of serials may be necessary to maintain effective control of aviation assets. For example, due to METT-TC considerations, it may be difficult to control 16 aircraft as a single serial. However, a lift of 16 aircraft with four serials of 4 aircraft each can be more easily controlled.

6-18. Multiple serials may also be necessary when the capacity of available PZs or LZs is limited. If available PZs or LZs can accommodate only 4 aircraft in a lift of 16 aircraft, it is best to organize into four serials of four aircraft each.

6-19. Multiple serials are employed to take advantage of available air routes. If several acceptable air routes are available, the AATFC may choose to employ serials to avoid concentrating his force along one air route. If the commander wants all his forces to land simultaneously in a single LZ, he does so by having the serials converge at a common RP before landing. With a lift of 16 aircraft and four available air routes, the AATFC can use four serials of 4 aircraft each, with each serial using a different air route. Each time there is a new lift, a new serial begins. For example, within lift one, there are serials one through four. For each lift thereafter, serials start again with one.

CHALKS

6-20. A chalk comprises personnel and equipment designated to be moved by a specific aircraft. When planning the air movement, each aircraft within the lift is termed a chalk. For example, within a lift of 10, there are aircraft chalks 1 through 10. For each lift thereafter, there are also chalks 1 through 10. Each aircraft is accounted for within each lift.

6-21. Chalks must be designated within serials just as they are within lifts. Counting within the serials is continuous up to the total number of aircraft in the lift. For example, in a lift of 16 aircraft in lift 1, serial 1, there are chalks 1 through 4. In lift 1, serial 2, there are chalks 5 through 8. In lift 1, serial 3, there are chalks 9 through 12. Finally, in lift 1, serial 4, there are chalks 13 through 16.

BUMP PLAN

6-22. The bump plan ensures that the most essential personnel and equipment arrive on time at the objective area. It specifies personnel and equipment that may be bumped from an aircraft or serial and delivered later. Each aircraft load and serial has a bump plan sequence designated on its air movement table. Figure 6-4 depicts an example of bump plan information.

Line #	Avn Unit	Lifted Unit	Lift	Serial	Chalk	PZ	PZ Arr/ Load Time	T/O Time	SP	RP	LZ	LZ Time	Load PAX	Load Sling	Remarks
1	2-344	A/1-603 IN	2	1	1-4	Maple	H-2+00:00	H-44:40	H-40:21	H-01:38	Robin	H+02:58	4x11 (44)		Bump 4
2	2-344	A/1-603 IN	2	2	5-8	Maple	H-2+00:00	H-43:40	H-39:21	H+02:38	Robin	H+03:58	4x11 (44)		
3	2-344	A/1-603 IN	2	3	9-12	Maple	H-2+00:00	H-42:40	H-38:21	H+03:38	Robin	H+04:58	4x11 (44)		Bump 12
4	2-344	A/1-603 IN, HHC 1-603 IN	2	4	13-16	Maple	H-2+00:00	H-41:40	H-37:21	H+04:38	Robin	H+05:58	4x11 (44)		Chalk 13 is the TAC CP

Figure 6-4. Example aircraft bump information

6-23. If all personnel within the chalk cannot be lifted, individuals must know who is to off-load and in what sequence. This ensures that key personnel are not bumped arbitrarily. This also ensures that key aircraft chalks are not left in the PZ. When an aircraft within a serial or flight cannot lift off and key personnel are onboard, they off-load and board another aircraft that has priority.

6-24. Bumped personnel report to a PZ bump area specified by company or larger units. At this location, they are accounted for, regrouped, and rescheduled by the PZCO for later delivery to appropriate LZs. Sometimes, spare aircraft are held in reserve for bumped chalks in the event a primary mission aircraft is unable to fly due to maintenance or other reasons. These spare aircraft remain staged on the PZ for occasions such as these or to fly other high priority serials.

SECTION II – STAGING PLAN

6-25. The staging plan organizes the movement of Soldiers and loads into position for the forthcoming air assault. It establishes the PZ and specifies the manner in which the supported unit organizes to execute the loading plan. The staging plan prescribes the arrival of ground units at the PZ in the proper order for movement. It prescribes what actions the ground unit must complete to prepare to load the aircraft. All vehicles and equipment to be lifted should be properly configured, inspected, and ready to load before the aircraft arrive at the PZ. Typically, ground units arrive at the PZ and posture in proper chalk order before their aircraft arrive.

6-26. Considerations for developing a staging plan follow.

PREPARATION FOR LOADING

6-27. Preparations for loading are typically conducted in a unit assembly area or other secure location that is near the PZ. Prior to reporting to the PZ, units complete all preparations to successfully load the aircraft, to include—

- Completing the air loading table or manifest. The chalk leaders verify the air loading table to ensure it is properly completed, making any changes to the manifest before arriving to the PZ.
- Preparing and inspecting all equipment for loading. The chalk leader's pre-rig all equipment to be sling loaded and ensure vehicles have the proper equipment to rig and fly. The chalk leaders inspect their loads and complete all necessary inspection records, to include DA Form 7382 (*Sling Load Inspection Record*), in accordance with FM 4-20.197.
- Conducting rehearsals for loading and off-loading the aircraft.

MOVEMENT TO PICKUP ZONE

6-28. Once units have completed preparations for loading, they begin movement to the PZ in accordance with the air movement table so that the Soldiers to load and the helicopter to be loaded arrive at the PZ at the same time. This prevents congestion, preserves security, and reduces vulnerability to enemy actions on the PZ.

6-29. To coordinate the movement of units to the PZ, the PZCO—

- Determines movement time of ground units to the PZ.
- Specifies arrival time(s) and sees that movement of units remains on schedule.

CHALK CHECK-IN AND INSPECTION

6-30. Upon arriving to the PZ area, the unit first checks in with the PZ control party at chalk check-in. The PZCO should plan adequate time for check-in based on mission variables. As a rule, the greater the number of serials in a lift, the longer it takes check-in and inspection for loading. Serials with large numbers of vehicles and equipment to be sling loaded also require more time to check in.

CHALK CHECK-IN

6-31. As the unit arrives at the check-in point, loads are identified by lift-serial-chalk. Chalk leaders are briefed, and their air loading tables or manifests are inspected. The chalk leader provides one copy of the manifest to the PZ control party.

LOAD WEIGH-IN

6-32. The loads are then weighed with all personnel and equipment to ensure they meet the allowable cargo loads (ACLs) as briefed in the AMB. Loads that are overweight are sent to a designated frustrated cargo area to download equipment prior to being reweighed.

LOAD INSPECTION

6-33. All items to be loaded are inspected in accordance with FM 4-20.197. For emergency purposes only, the PZ control party may maintain a parts box for on-the-spot corrections. Units are responsible for the serviceability and corrective maintenance of their own equipment.

6-34. Loads with deficiencies are sent to a designated frustrated cargo area. Loads must remain in the frustrated area until deficiencies are corrected and the loads are inspected again. No load is allowed to leave the frustrated area without permission from the PZCO.

LOAD STAGING

6-35. Once a serial is complete, a chalk guide from the PZ control leads it into position on the PZ. Loads are staged in reverse chalk order by serial in accordance with the PZ diagram.

6-36. Once the chalk is staged and in PZ posture, the chalk leader should brief his chalk on—

- Seating arrangement.
- Loading procedures.
- Use of safety belts.
- In-flight procedures.
- Off-loading procedures.

SLING LOAD OPERATIONS

6-37. The three phases of a sling load operation are—

- **Preparation and rigging.** Loads are prepared and rigged in accordance with FM 4-20.197 or unit standing operating procedure.

- **Inspection.** A Pathfinder School graduate, Sling Load Inspector Certification Course graduate, or an Air Assault School graduate in the rank of Specialist and above is qualified to inspect and certify each load. The individual who rigged the load cannot inspect the same load. The contents of the load are recorded on a DA Form 7382.
- **Sling load operation.** Trained ground crews hook up loads.

SLING LOAD UNITS

6-38. The three different elements involved in a sling load operation are the supported unit, the aviation unit, and the receiving unit. In an air assault, the supported unit and the receiving unit are typically the same. The responsibilities of each element are as described below:

- Supported unit is responsible for—
    - Selecting, preparing, and controlling the PZ.
    - Requisitioning all the equipment needed for sling load operations.
    - Inspecting and maintaining all sling load equipment.
    - Providing trained ground crews for rigging and inspecting, filing inspection forms, controlling aircraft, aircraft guides, hooking up loads, and clearing the aircraft for departure.
    - Providing load dispositions and instructions to the aviation unit for the sling load equipment.
    - Verifying the load weight (to include rigging equipment).
- Aviation unit is responsible for—
    - Establishing coordination with the supported unit.
    - Advising the supported unit on load limitations.
    - Advising the supported units on the suitability of selected LZs and PZs.
    - Providing assistance in the recovery and return of sling load equipment.
    - Establishing safety procedures and understanding of duties and responsibility between the flight crew and ground crew.
- Receiving unit is responsible for—
    - Selecting, preparing, and controlling the LZ.
    - Providing trained ground crews to guide the aircraft and de-rig the loads.
    - Coordinating for the control and return of the sling load equipment.
    - Inspecting the rigging of back loads (sling load equipment returning to PZ).

SLING LOAD TEAMS

6-39. Three personnel are normally used for the ground crew in external load operations on the PZ and LZ: a signal person, a static probe person, and a hook-up person.

6-40. The static probe person carries an electricity probe consisting of an insulated contact rod joined by a length of metallic tape or electrical wire to a ground rod. All ground crew personnel wear the following protective equipment:

- Advanced Combat Helmet with chinstrap fastened.
- Goggles.
- Earplugs.
- Gloves.
- Sleeves rolled down and buttoned.
- Identification card and tags.

HOOK-UP PROCEDURES

6-41. The aircraft approaches the hook-up site, and the signal person guides it into position over the load. The static probe person drives the ground rod into the ground and discharges the static electricity from the aircraft by holding the contact rod, which is connected to the ground rod, to the cargo hook of the aircraft. The hook-up person then attaches the apex fitting to the aircraft cargo hook.

RELEASE PROCEDURES

6-42. The aircraft approaches the release site, and the signal person guides it into position. The hook-up release team stands by but is not actively employed unless the slings cannot be released from the aircraft. Normally, the ground crew at the LZ consists of one signal person and two release personnel.

GROUND CREW EMERGENCY PROCEDURES

In an emergency, the ground crew moves to a predesignated rendezvous point identified by prior coordination with the aviation unit.

This page intentionally left blank.

Chapter 7

Augmenting Air Assaults

Air assaults are combined arms operations requiring the integration of all AATF members. Planning and executing a successful air assault involves careful consideration of the many tasks that make up air assault support.

SECTION I – ATTACK RECONNAISSANCE BATTALION AND SQUADRON SUPPORT

7-1.   The attack reconnaissance battalion and squadron both bring firepower, speed, and shock effect to an air assault operation. During a large scale air assault, the higher headquarters may employ these units under command of a CAB, or they may be OPCON to an AATF for a BCT or smaller air assault. Air assaults always include attack reconnaissance aviation supporting the AATF. Table 7-1 lists the attack reconnaissance battalion and squadron units found in the CAB.

Table 7-1. Attack reconnaissance battalion and squadron assets

Unit	Assets	Companies/Troops	A/C Availability Planning Figures
Attack reconnaissance battalion	24 AH-64s	3	18
Attack reconnaissance squadron	30 OH-58s	3	24

AIRCRAFT ALLOCATIONS

7-2.   The typical allocation of attack helicopters to a BCT-sized AATF is one attack helicopter task force. The normal command relationship is OPCON to the AATF. The AATF may assume OPCON of the air reconnaissance battalion or attack reconnaissance squadron as much as 96 hours and at least 24 hours prior to the air assault for planning and preparation. An attack reconnaissance squadron may also be OPCON to a BCT air assault operation either in addition to or in lieu of the air reconnaissance battalion. For this discussion, attack aviation refers to both the attack reconnaissance battalion and attack reconnaissance squadron fighting in the attack role.

AH-64 EMPLOYMENT

7-3.   The AATF should employ attack aircraft in teams (two aircraft) or platoons (four aircraft). Employing the AH-64 in a company-sized element provides a good balance of capabilities in terms of—

- Conducting aerial reconnaissance in the AO.
- Massing fires to destroy up to a battalion-sized mechanized force (or equivalent).
- Conducting distributed attack aviation operations in up to three separate locations to maintain a continuous presence.

7-4.   The AH-64 is normally employed as two-aircraft teams if the requirement for continuous presence outweighs the requirements for massed firepower. The company, however, is the lowest level that plans and coordinates operations. During an air assault, the AMC controls the attack aviation elements until the air assault is completed. Once ground forces are established in the LZ, attack aviation units establish communications with the ground elements and prepare to provide security and execute CCA as necessary.

7-5.   Typically, attack aviation is employed in support of an air assault prior to commitment of the ground tactical force to conduct shaping operations in order to set the conditions for air assault execution. In order to better coordinate and synchronize operations, the higher headquarters may consolidate all attack aviation units under one CAB during shaping operations. Time-sensitive or smaller than battalion-level air assault operations may have reduced timelines for shaping operations or may not require shaping operations at all based on the mission variables.

7-6. Prior to air assault execution, the attack reconnaissance battalion conducts terrain- and force-oriented reconnaissance as early as possible up to commitment of the ground tactical force. The purpose of this reconnaissance is to—

- Destroy high-value targets of opportunity.
- Confirm or deny the suitability of air routes and LZs.
- Gain information on the ground routes from the LZs to the objectives.
- Gain information on the objective area.

7-7. The attack aviation elements begin to confirm or deny the enemy disposition and destroy select high-value targets. The focus of shaping operations is reconnaissance. A shift to emphasize attack operations exclusively, usually to destroy an enemy force of great criticality, requires a deliberate decision by the AATFC. Upon completion of the reconnaissance, the attack aviation elements provide the reconnaissance products to the AATFC for his assessment.

7-8. Just prior to execution of the air assault, attack aviation operations focus on completing shaping operations for the air assault and then transitions to providing security and CCA fires for the air assault. After the initial lift is in, the focus of the attack aviation shifts to providing supporting fires for the GTC. A typical pattern for attack helicopter operations prior to air assault execution begins with attacks to destroy known enemy forces that can affect the air assault to complete shaping operations. This is normally an aviation company operation. This stage ends with the LZs confirmed cold and with attack aviation units in overwatch positions prepared to deliver precision aerial fires in support of the landing plan. Typically, the lead company conducts a battle handover to a second company who performs the actual overwatch. This second company overwatches the initial lift into each LZ and then either pushes out beyond the LZ to conduct security operations or provides CCA for the GTC. The third company usually cycles in to extend the duration of the security mission and supporting fires.

7-9. If the LZs are hot, the AATFC may decide to delay, divert, or abort the mission. Actions by the AATFC and attack reconnaissance aviation may be the only way to achieve a cold LZ status. The attack aviation elements provide an estimate of the time and resources required to achieve a cold status. This requires close coordination between the AATFC and attack aviation elements to avoid fratricide and to minimize risk to the aircrews.

7-10. For planning purposes, an attack reconnaissance helicopter company or troop can perform no more than one task at a time. Depending on the duration of a particular task, attack reconnaissance companies or troops may be able to conduct two tasks sequentially as long as they are related efforts (for example, transitioning from LZ overwatch to LZ security or CCA). The limiting factor for conducting sequential tasks is crew endurance.

AIR ASSAULT SECURITY

7-11. Another common mission conducted by the air reconnaissance battalion during an air assault is air assault security. The air assault security force protects lift and assault forces from the PZ to the LZ to preserve combat power. Air assault security is not an escort mission.

- The first attack team departs in advance of the assault force and flies along the same route it will use. Subsequent teams use separate routes so as not to conflict with subsequent lifts.
- Teams initially conduct force-oriented reconnaissance in vicinity of the LZ.
- Priority of the reconnaissance effort is to identify any air defense artillery systems or direct fire weapons that could influence the air assault.
- At the set time listed on the execution checklist (usually not later than RP plus 2 minutes), the attack element provides an LZ update and calls either HOT or COLD for the LZ. If the LZ is hot, the element makes an estimate of the assets required and how long it would take to turn the condition to cold.

- Prior to the arrival of the assault force, priority of indirect fires are generally given to the attack element on station. Upon arrival at the LZ, the GTC assumes priority of fire.
- Attack reconnaissance aircraft provide security by integrating into the ground tactical plan and responding to all encountered threats. Stationary support- and attack-by-fire positions are not desirable for attack aviation elements, and deliberate AC2 integration is required to ensure precision aerial fires are available during the assault.

OH-58 EMPLOYMENT

7-12. The attack reconnaissance squadron is organized into three troops of 10 aircraft each (8 for planning). The attack reconnaissance squadron uses two aircraft teams, whole troops, or the entire squadron to execute missions. Generally, a team can conduct any of the subtasks under the basic task of reconnaissance. For security missions, it requires more than just one team per subtask.

7-13. Based on other mission requirements, the attack reconnaissance squadron can support a BCT air assault with the entire squadron or any portion of troops or teams required. If the entire squadron supports the mission, a C2 element goes forward with the air assault commander, squadron commander, or S-3 riding in the C2 aircraft. A task organization with both attack reconnaissance squadron and attack reconnaissance battalion units provides the greatest versatility to maximize aircraft capabilities and best serves the AATFC.

7-14. During air assault operations, the attack reconnaissance squadron is best suited to perform the basic task of zone reconnaissance and CCAs for the AATFC. These missions help the AATFC determine how to allocate attack assets to destroy the enemy and assist in course of action development through the location and determination of suitable LZs. Reconnaissance products (video, LZ sketches, and other imagery) also assist planning operations in and around the LZ(s). The attack reconnaissance squadron may also conduct interdiction attacks and air assault security. However, as with the attack reconnaissance battalion performing reconnaissance, these missions do not maximize the use of aircraft capabilities.

7-15. Prior to air assault execution, the squadron conducts shaping operations, which usually consist of terrain-oriented reconnaissance and force-oriented reconnaissance. Both types of reconnaissance assist the commander in determining if the shaping operations have set the conditions for execution of the air assault.

- **Terrain-oriented reconnaissance** involves reconnoitering possible forward arming and refueling point (FARP) sites, the objective, possible attack aviation positions, deception objectives, and primary and alternate LZs to determine suitability. The squadron may also conduct route reconnaissance to validate air routes and determine if enemy air defense systems can influence movement along the routes. If any enemies are found, the squadron develops the situation and provides information for the commander. Mission variables determine whether the squadron uses supporting fires (artillery or close air support), organic fires or passes the target to attack aviation assets to destroy.
- **Force-oriented reconnaissance** involves identifying remaining enemy elements in the operational area that may influence the air assault.

7-16. During the conduct of the air assault, the attack reconnaissance squadron may perform one or more of the following missions:

- **Air route reconnaissance** to determine suitability of air routes into and out of the objective areas.
- **Air route security** to prevent the enemy from influencing movement along the air route (s). This task may include establishing the forward passage lane for follow-on attack or lift assets, hasty attacks, and so on.
- **Area security** to deny enemy the ability to influence friendly actions in the vicinity of the LZ (s) or objective(s). This task may include establishing observation posts to overwatch the LZ(s), providing LZ updates, establishing a screen, CCAs, and reconnaissance of ground routes from LZ to objective. If indirect and SEAD fires are preplanned, the timeline should allow sufficient time for the aircraft on station to determine if the LZ is hot or cold. Attack reconnaissance aircraft provide security by integrating into the AC2 plan and responding to all encountered threats. Stationary support- or attack-by-fire positions are not desirable for attack aviation

elements, and deliberate AC2 integration is required to effectively ensure precision aerial fires are available during the assault.

● **Area or zone reconnaissance** to determine suitability of LZs and enemy disposition on objective areas as well as terrain that can influence LZs and objectives.

● **Screen** to prevent the enemy from surprising friendly forces in the vicinity of the LZ(s) or objective(s). A security zone may be established outside of the objective area to trigger attack assets or closer in to assist the ground maneuver elements.

7-17. The squadron may also perform other missions during or immediately following the air assault, to include reconnaissance of follow-on objectives, other security operations, route reconnaissance and security, and more. Throughout these missions, the squadron is prepared to conduct target and battle handovers to attack aviation elements and CCAs, assist with C2, and provide reconnaissance information and products.

SECTION II – GROUND RECONNAISSANCE SUPPORT

7-18. Each of the different BCTs has its own organic reconnaissance capabilities. These include a reconnaissance squadron in each BCT and a reconnaissance platoon in each of the maneuver battalions within the BCTs. The HBCT and SBCT also have a CBRN platoon that is capable of conducting CBRN reconnaissance to determine the presence and extent of CBRN contamination. The SBCT also has a ground sensor platoon which provides remotely emplaced unmanned monitoring capabilities.

7-19. Each reconnaissance squadron's organization and equipment are slightly different, but they all are capable of conducting reconnaissance and security missions throughout the BCTs AO. (See FM 3-20.96, for details.) The objective of ground reconnaissance is to support the AATF reconnaissance and security plan by collecting information about the enemy (to include locations of enemy forces), conducting reconnaissance of planned LZs and objectives, and maintaining surveillance of assigned areas of interest.

7-20. The main difference between the reconnaissance elements of the BCTs is that the Infantry brigade combat team and their organic vehicles are deployable by rotary-wing assets, whereas the reconnaissance elements of the HBCT or SBCT and their organic vehicles are not. This does not preclude the employment of the HBCT and SBCT reconnaissance elements without their vehicles or mean that they are less capable than their Infantry brigade combat team counterparts, but it is a factor to consider when planning an air assault in an HBCT or SBCT. The accompanying situation that confronts planners in an HBCT and SBCT is linking up the reconnaissance units with their vehicles.

INSERTION AND EXTRACTION

7-21. The reconnaissance unit plans for an air insertion or extraction as it does for any other mission. In addition to the normal planning process, specific planning requirements that exist for the air insertion include—

● Coordinating with the supporting aviation unit(s) of the task force.

● Planning and rehearsing with the supporting aviation unit prior to the mission if possible.

● Gathering as much information as possible about the enemy situation in preparation for the mission.

● Ensuring joint SEAD coordination as appropriate.

7-22. Reconnaissance units may be air inserted and extracted in preplanned LZs and PZs by helicopter to accomplish their mission. The aircraft required to insert and extract a reconnaissance unit depends on the size and type of equipment with which the unit is organized but typically consists of UH-60s or UH-47s and AH-64s or OH-58s.The supporting aviation unit typically conducts multiple false insertions before and after the actual insertion.

7-23. Some terrain may not allow helicopter landings. In these cases, reconnaissance units may be inserted or extracted while the helicopters hover over the unsuitable landing areas. Reconnaissance personnel may require the Special Patrol Insertion/Extraction System (SPIES) or Fast-Rope Insertion/Extraction System

(FRIES) equipment and additional training and rehearsals to successfully conduct these techniques. (See FM 3-05.210 for details on SPIES and FRIES.)

7-24. If reconnaissance units do not have follow-on missions, they may be extracted from the objective area. Reconnaissance units typically plan for normal, emergency, and lost communication extraction points. A preplanned extraction point requires the unit to verify the planned pickup time and location. If a situation arises that requires emergency extraction of the reconnaissance unit, communication and coordination is made to establish an emergency pickup time window. The lost communication extraction point requires units to move to a preplanned emergency extraction point after two consecutive missed communication windows and wait for pickup in accordance with orders or standing operating procedures.

EMPLOYMENT

7-25. Reconnaissance units conduct traditional reconnaissance missions as part of the shaping operations to help create and preserve the conditions to execute an air assault. Once inserted, a reconnaissance unit conducts a tactical movement to its assigned AO and begins its assigned mission, which may include one or all of the following missions:

- **Area or zone reconnaissance.** The reconnaissance unit conducts reconnaissance of planned LZ(s) and objective area(s) to gain information on the terrain and to provide detailed information on the disposition of enemy forces. This may be an assigned mission if the GTC decides to utilize the reconnaissance unit to select, identify, mark, and set up an LZ or PZ.
- **Route reconnaissance.** The reconnaissance unit conducts reconnaissance of planned route or axis to gain information on the terrain surrounding the route that the enemy may use to impede movement on the route. This may be an assigned mission if the GTC wants to use a specific route from the LZ to the objective.
- **Screen.** The reconnaissance unit conducts a screen of the LZ or objective area to provide early warning of enemy approach and to provide information, reaction time, and maneuver space for the ground force. This may be an assigned mission if the GTC wants continuous surveillance of the LZ or objective areas to provide early warning of enemy approach or to report enemy activity.

7-26. Attack aviation elements conduct shaping operations at the LZs and objective areas in coordination with reconnaissance units. Reconnaissance units and attack aircraft coordinate to ensure the aircraft know the location of the reconnaissance units. To aid in the prevention of fratricide, the reconnaissance units coordinate no-fire areas for their locations in the LZ or objective area and locate in the no-fire areas prior to employing CCA. The reconnaissance units coordinate their preplanned no-fire areas with their FSO, who ensures the no-fire areas are given to the AATF FSO. An alternate plan is to have the reconnaissance units move to a no-fire area away from the LZ or objective before the attack aviation elements arrive on station and conduct call-for-fire missions to vector the aircraft to targets. If the reconnaissance units require close support from attack aviation, they implement the attack helicopter CCA request for support procedure. (See Chapter 4 for details on CCA requests.)

SECTION III – PATHFINDER SUPPORT

7-27. Pathfinder units are organic to certain CABs (for example, the 101st CAB and 159th CAB from the 101st Air Assault Division and the 82d CAB of the 82d Airborne Division). However, they may be requested by the AATF from their higher headquarters to support the air assault mission. They should be requested as soon as receiving an order to conduct an air assault so that they may be integrated into the air assault plan. Pathfinder availability, complexity of the operation, terrain, and air assault proficiency of the supported ground unit are some common factors that may dictate the level of pathfinder support. In most operations, three to six Soldiers comprise the pathfinder element that supports an air assault of a BCT or smaller-sized element. (See FM 3-21.38 for details on pathfinder operations.)

7-28. Pathfinders provide navigational assistance and air traffic advisories for fixed- and rotary-wing aircraft that encompass selecting, improving, marking, and controlling the PZ or LZ that supports any phase of an air assault operation. They may also perform limited physical improvement and CBRN monitoring and surveying within LZs.

INSERTION AND EXTRACTION

7-29. Pathfinders may be inserted in a variety of modes, to include—

- **Helicopter.** Pathfinders may be inserted into preplanned LZs by helicopter as early as possible prior to execution of the air assault. Upon insertion, the pathfinders infiltrate to the planned LZs and begin their mission. If the terrain does not allow helicopter landings, the pathfinders may rappel or fast-rope while the helicopters hover over the unsuitable landing areas. Pathfinders can also be inserted using the SPIES or FRIES.
- **Parachute.** Pathfinders may parachute from fixed- or rotary-wing aircraft. The best time to insert by parachute is at night during a low or non-illuminated period to maximize secrecy.
- **Infiltration.** This is the least preferred method because it is slow and requires a long lead time for the pathfinders to reach their assigned AO.

7-30. Typically, the pathfinders are extracted on the first aircraft of the last lift into the LZ or conduct an exfiltration from the area on foot and conduct follow-on missions. If the pathfinders are going to conduct follow-on missions, those missions are normally planned prior to the initial insertion. If the pathfinder team fails to make two consecutive communication windows, they move to a preplanned PZ where they wait for extraction. Pathfinders initiate their ground evasion plan in accordance with the unit standing operating procedure if they are not extracted within the allotted time.

7-31. Pathfinders initiate an emergency extraction when they are compromised or cannot continue their mission. The pathfinders notify the AATF CP that an emergency extraction is required, break contact, and move to a precoordinated PZ for extraction. The AATF notifies the assault helicopter unit to initiate the extraction. An assault helicopter unit normally conducts the extraction with AH-64s and UH-60s. The AATF FSO executes a preplanned SEAD mission to support the extraction mission.

EMPLOYMENT

7-32. If the operation is conducted in daylight, the pathfinders are inserted before the initial assault force only if the commander suspects that the LZ may require improvement. Once they are in position, they send back the conditions, suitability, and enemy situation on the LZs and continue to observe the primary LZs for changing situations. The primary and alternate LZs are confirmed for suitability, and the information is relayed back to the AATF CP. Once the LZs are confirmed, the pathfinders start setting up the LZ using red-colored panels or other easily-identifiable means to mark any hard-to-detect, impossible-to-remove obstacles, such as wires, holes, stumps, and rocks.

7-33. If an operation is during limited visibility, pathfinders arrive before the main body does. As soon as they arrive, the pathfinders reconnoiter the LZ, begin setting the LZ up by marking the landing direction and landing points and any obstacles within the landing site that they cannot reduce or remove, and establish air traffic control. If the tactical situation does not allow the marking of obstacles, the pathfinders advise the supporting aviation unit. Soldiers from the supported ground unit may accompany the pathfinders. These additional Soldiers provide security for the pathfinders and help them clear any obstacles on the LZ.

7-34. After the LZ is set up and marked, the pathfinders maintain surveillance on the LZs until they are required to move to and mark the RP if the LZ is on or next to the objective. For LZs away from the objective, the pathfinders provide terminal guidance for the assault aircraft to the LZ. While executing terminal guidance, the pathfinders establish no-fire areas and locate in the no-fire areas when attack aircraft are on station. It is imperative that the aircraft maintain communication with the pathfinders to confirm the location and movements of the pathfinders on the ground.

7-35. The primary means of communication for the pathfinders is single-channel tactical satellite, followed by VHF radios and HF radios. To keep radio transmissions to a minimum and to conserve battery power, the pathfinders commonly use communications windows while on missions. The communications window is established in the operation order. The communication window is the opportunity for the inserted team(s) to send important information to the AATF CP. This information can include enemy activity, enemy contact, resupply requests, and so on. If communication is not made, the team works on their communications problem throughout the communication window.

SECTION IV – FIRES PLANNING AND COORDINATION

7-36. Responsive, lethal indirect fires for air assault operations depend heavily on the use of mortars and 105- and 155-mm howitzers that are air assaulted into the LZ or to another location within range of the objective or LZ. Because of the distance at which most air assaults occur, these are the only organic all-weather indirect FS assets that provide close supporting fires, effective counterfire, or lengthy suppressive fires. A fires brigade's rocket and missile fires may also support an air assault, particularly for long-range SEAD targets.

ALLOCATIONS

7-37. The artillery support for a BCT-sized AATF is normally the fires battalion assigned to the BCT. Because a BCT AATF normally flows into LZs as battalion-sized maneuver elements, the fires battalion's batteries and platoons typically air assault into their own LZ. Other fires battalion assets, such as the Q-36 radar, fires battalion C2, and survey section, may be task organized with a battery or platoon or a maneuver battalion for air movement into the AO. The exact composition of artillery units air assaulted in support of a BCT-sized or battalion AATF is dependent on the mission variables.

7-38. The 155-mm artillery provides increased range, lethality, and ammunition options. Because 155-mm artillery and Q-37 radar air assault separate from their prime movers, they may require dedicated LZs that are reconnoitered and prepared by pathfinders or other reconnaissance elements prior to air movement. Once on the LZ, they are largely immobile and more vulnerable to enemy artillery, air, or ground attacks until their prime movers linkup by ground convoy.

EMPLOYMENT

7-39. A firing battery or platoon requires adequate ammunition to provide sufficient FS to the AATFC. The planning factors for artillery air assaults outlined below provide for a specific, minimal quantity of ammunition. Additional aircraft may be required to sling in artillery ammunition with the initial assault force or planned for the follow-on resupply depending on METT-TC analysis.

7-40. A 105-mm fires battalion basic load is approximately 3,700 rounds. The 155-mm battery basic load is approximately 1,500 rounds. While a complete basic load is not always required to support an air assault operation, these numbers provide a starting point for artillery ammunition planning.

7-41. The three primary techniques to use when employing air assault artillery are—
- Offset firing unit (deliberate air assault).
- Accompanying firing unit (deliberate air assault).
- Artillery raid.

7-42. Each technique offers distinct advantages and disadvantages. In any given air assault operation, one or more of these techniques may be employed. For example, an artillery raid may be used prior to the BCT air assault, in conjunction with the attack aviation shaping operation, to neutralize an enemy air defense artillery site that impacts on the attack aviation scheme of maneuver. An offset firing unit may then be used to provide preparatory fires on the air assault objective and close support to the first lifts into the LZ. The battalion uses the remainder of the fires in the accompanying firing unit technique to provide close support to the BCT AATF as it lands in the LZ and executes the ground tactical plan.

OFFSET FIRING UNIT TECHNIQUE

7-43. The offset firing unit technique consists of a deliberate air assault of a firing battery into a position offset or away from the objective or LZ before arrival of the main force. This technique is used when FS is needed in the LZ or objective for an extended period of time and available prior to or immediately at the start of an operation.

7-44. The larger the inserted element becomes, the more difficult it becomes to control. One technique is to insert a small C2 element from the fires battalion with the battery to coordinate security and any missions. The C2 element coordinates with the AATF headquarters, thus allowing the battery commander to focus on firing battery operations.

7-45. The decision to air assault the 105-mm battery or platoon with or without prime movers is METT-TC dependent. Having prime movers provides additional flexibility and sustainment and is generally preferred. Lack of suitable aircraft or the assessment that the potential need to move the battery is low may permit the use of this option. The unit needs its prime movers if survivability moves are anticipated.

ACCOMPANYING FIRING UNIT TECHNIQUE

7-46. The accompanying firing unit technique consists of a deliberate air assault of one or more firing batteries or platoons simultaneously with the arrival of the assault force. This technique is used when FS is needed in the LZ or objective for an extended period of time and other units can provide immediate FS for the assault force until the battery is established.

ARTILLERY RAID TECHNIQUE

7-47. The artillery raid technique consists of air assaulting a firing element forward to fire a specific mission and then extracting the element via helicopter immediately after the mission is completed. This is usually done as a mission separate from a maneuver air assault but may be used as an alternative to the offset firing unit technique based on mission variables. The artillery raid technique is used when a stationary, high-value target requires attack by indirect fires, the fires are needed for a short time only, and adequate observation of the target is provided. Quick and timely execution is of the essence. Target analysis determines the number of howitzers and the amount of ammunition required for the raid. Actual equipment and personnel required is METT-TC dependent.

7-48. The air assault artillery raid is a high-risk operation of short duration used to allow the attack of high-payoff targets located beyond the range of friendly artillery and targets tactically out of range of other available FS or maneuver systems. Detailed planning, accurate fires of sufficient volume, and speed in execution are key to its success.

7-49. Both the M119 (105-mm) and the M777 (155-mm) howitzers can be used to conduct an air assault artillery raid. The M119 can be rigged as an external load or internal load, and the M777 can be rigged externally. While the available aircraft may limit some of the configuration choices, the battery commander normally determines the most suitable configuration based on mission variables and in coordination with the artillery S-3 and AMC.

SECTION V – MEDICAL EVACUATION

7-50. Medical evacuation refers to both ground and air evacuation of casualties. Air medical evacuation employs air assets from the air ambulance companies assigned to the CAB and general support aviation battalions to evacuate casualties. The nine-line MEDEVAC request is the standard method to request MEDEVAC.

7-51. Casualty evacuation refers to the use of nonmedical tracked or wheeled vehicles or aircraft to evacuate casualties. Casualty evacuation should only be used when the number of casualties exceeds the capability of the MEDEVAC assets (such as in a mass casualty situation) or when the urgency of evacuation exceeds the risk of waiting for MEDEVAC assets to arrive. Typically, both air and ground evacuation is planned for air assaults.

PLANNING CONSIDERATIONS

7-52. The CAB allocates MEDEVAC assets to the supported AATF for the duration of the air assault. However, the size and distance of the planned air assault dictates the duration of MEDEVAC support to the AATFC. As a general rule, the supporting commander should provide MEDEVAC assets to the supported commander until ground lines of communications are established.

7-53. Typically, the evacuation platoon leader from the brigade support medical company and the air ambulance platoon leader from the air ambulance company conduct the MEDEVAC planning for air assaults. They do so in coordination with the AATF S-1, AATF S-4, BAE, AATF S-3, supported unit S-3,

BCT surgeon section, and BCT support medical company commander. The air ambulance platoon leader should brief the MEDEVAC plan at the AMCM, AMB, and health service support rehearsal.

7-54. When planning for MEDEVAC during an air assault—

- Integrate ground evacuation measures into the overall MEDEVAC plan.
- Plan MEDEVAC routes to Level II or III health care facilities. Ensure routes are briefed to all aircrews participating in the air assault.
- Plan for medical personnel to fly on casualty evacuation aircraft if time and situation permit.
- Ensure MEDEVAC crews are available for air assault orders, rehearsals, and preparations.
- Brief casualty collection point locations during the air assault rehearsal.
- Plan to maintain a FARP after the air assault is completed so that MEDEVAC aircraft have a place to stage from for follow-on ground tactical operations.

7-55. Medical evacuation aircraft are limited assets and should be scheduled and used accordingly. The air assault task force's casualty estimate provides planning guidance for the number of MEDEVAC aircraft needed to support air assaults. To maximize the amount of mission hours they can support the mission, MEDEVAC aircraft should be staged to support an air assault at the latest possible time. Medical evacuation aircraft should support short distance air assaults from the PZ or brigade support area. To expedite pick up of casualties in long distance air assaults, aircraft may stage at a FARP or use a ROZ.

EXECUTION

7-56. Medical and casualty evacuation aircraft are normally OPCON to the AATF during air assault operations. The AMC controls the MEDEVAC flights to facilitate quick deconfliction of airspace. The AMC clears all medical and casualty evacuation aircraft movements, to include launch and landings. The AATFC may retain launch authority, but the AMC is responsible for MEDEVAC execution.

7-57. Medical or casualty evacuation is typically requested over the CAN for the duration of the air assault operation until an evacuation net, if necessary, is established. This ensures good coordination for deconfliction of fires and airspace.

7-58. When executing MEDEVAC operations—

- Send MEDEVAC aircraft into secure LZs if possible.
- Integrate attack reconnaissance aviation units to provide escort and LZ overwatch as required.
- Ensure terminal guidance into the LZ.
- Ensure redundant means of communication with the supporting MEDEVAC assets throughout the air assault.
- Designate a MEDEVAC officer in charge, typically a medical officer from the brigade support medical company, to ride on C2 aircraft to receive and prioritize evacuation mission requests and forward this information to the AMC for launch.

CASUALTY BACKHAUL PROCEDURE

7-59. During air assault planning, the AATF staff and aviation unit staff plan the combined use of aerial and ground medical and casualty evacuation assets. While assaulting aircraft may backhaul wounded from the LZ, the time required to load and unload casualties could desynchronize the air movement table.

7-60. Executing casualty evacuation during an air assault may cause delays in air assault missions unless spare aircraft are committed to replace aircraft designated to backhaul casualties. Designating separate casualty evacuation aircraft may prevent delays of follow-on lifts.

7-61. The typical procedure for casualty backhaul during air assaults follows:

(1) MEDEVAC request goes to C2 aircraft. The medical officer onboard relays the request to the AMC. If the request is approved, the AMC directs the next serial's last two aircraft (per mission variables), after dropping off personnel, to move to the LZ casualty collection point to pick up casualties.

(2) All backhauled casualties are taken back to the PZ casualty collection point.

(3) Backhaul aircraft with casualties notify PZ control they are inbound with casualties.

(4) If necessary, the last serial of the final lift makes the final pick up of casualties before the conclusion of the air assault.

LANDING ZONE PROCEDURES

7-62. The preferred methods of marking LZs during an air medical evacuation follow:

- Day: smoke (do not activate until instructed) or VS-17 panel marker.
- Night: strobe or swinging infrared chemlight (any color except blue or green that are not visible under night vision goggles).

7-63. Other general considerations for LZ procedures are—

- Select LZs that are level and clear of debris within a 50-meter radius.
- Keep all other light sources away from the LZ unless instructed otherwise by aircrew.
- Once MEDEVAC aircraft are inbound, make an estimated time-of-arrival call. The person communicating with the aircraft at the pickup site should have visual on the LZ to confirm the signal or to assist the crew as required.
- Once MEDEVAC aircraft have landed, keep personnel away from the aircraft while the medic comes to the patient. The unit should provide personnel to assist in loading the patient on the aircraft under direction of the medic.

SECTION VI – SUSTAINMENT OPERATIONS

7-64. An air assault is unique in that it routinely operates over extended distances that often preclude the normal throughput of supplies via standard ground lines of communications. Therefore, aerial resupply must be employed using rotary-wing aircraft. For rotary-wing aerial resupply, the sustainment operations concept allows for the timely distribution of supplies while simultaneously maximizing both aircraft and unit support capabilities. The AATF coordinates with its assigned brigade sustainment battalion. The same rules apply when units are operating at smaller outposts supported by battalion- or company-level assets.

CONCEPT OF OPERATIONS

7-65. Each BSB executes sustainment operations in their respective support area to receive and send loads. In preparation for sustainment operations, the sustainment brigade support operations section conducts an AMCM within 72 hours of any BCT or larger operation.

7-66. This meeting is chaired by the sustainment brigade support operations officer (SPO). Attendees include—

- Representatives from the support operations section of each BSB.
- All supported unit S-4s.
- Commodity managers.
- Transportation section.
- CAB representatives.

7-67. Issues discussed at this conference include—

- Concept of sustainment operations and support.
- Task organization.
- Request for aviation support process.
- Communications.
- Liaison officer identification and location.
- Proposed sustainment locations.
- Aviation brigade concerns and issues.
- Sustainment brigade concerns and issues.

7-68. In order to adequately support a BCT-sized air assault, aircraft must be considered for distribution of sustainment in sufficient numbers to support follow-on logistic requirements. The CABs CH-47s are normally planned to move supplies and equipment from the BCT sustainment area forward to the supported battalion combat trains or logistics resupply points. In some instances, or in the event of emergency resupply, supplies may be moved from a higher headquarters sustainment area directly to forward positions. Based on mission variables, the higher headquarters commander allocates the necessary number and type of aircraft to the sustainment brigade for the aerial resupply effort. The sustainment brigade support operations section, working in conjunction with a CAB liaison officer, plans the effort of resupply to the BSB sustainment areas. For aerial distribution from the BSB sustainment area forward, mission planning and execution are the responsibility of the BSB SPO, in close coordination with the supporting aviation elements.

PREPARATION

7-69. The tempo of resupply operations can dramatically impact combat operations. It is essential to optimize aircraft utilization by maximizing the number of turns during each shift. When possible, conduct a rehearsal of sustainment operations. This usually consists of an actual hook up, load transport, and a fuel spill rehearsal. The supporting aviation unit provides aircraft and crews to conduct training for personnel who comprise hook-up teams. The sustainment officers in charge are responsible for supervising this training.

7-70. When establishing sustainment operations, consider the—
- PZ location, especially road networks to and from.
- PZ security.
- Size.
- Petroleum, oils, and lubricants spill plan.
- Aviation hazards in immediate vicinity.
- Approach and departure headings.
- Trafficability of terrain in poor weather.

AIR ASSAULT TASK FORCE SUSTAINMENT OPERATIONS

7-71. Units plan to air assault with supplies adequate for sustainment until additional logistic support can be established by air or ground. Forward logistics elements composition and logistic aircraft distribution within the AATF must take the mission variables and follow-on resupply plan into account.

7-72. At the beginning of sustainment operations, the BSB SPO receives support requirements from the AATF S-4 during the logistics meeting prior to the actual resupply operation. The AATF S-4 is responsible for consolidating and prioritizing the support requirements from the subordinate unit S-4s.

7-73. Platoon leaders prepare supplies for sling load operations in the BSB sustainment area based on the guidance from the AATF S-4 and the BSB SPO. The SPO plans resupply missions for the entire AATF based on input from the AATF S-4. The SPO makes the ultimate decision on how best to resupply units based on the situation. After support requirements have been identified, the SPO attends the AMCM.

7-74. The night before the planned resupply, the SPO conducts an AMB. Attendees include the—
- SPO.
- Aviation operations representatives (S-3 or pilots).
- Air assault task force S-4.
- Supported unit S-4s.
- Forward support company commanders or executive officers.

7-75. The sustainment officer in charge is responsible for developing the PZ diagram. The battalion S-4s and forward support company commanders are also responsible for developing the LZ diagrams and for coordinating and briefing the LZ security plans.

7-76. Forward support company commanders ensure that their resupply loads are prepared in the BSB sustainment area using their respective units' air items. When the resupply aircraft arrive, unit S-4s take control of the ground crews and the support platoon leaders fly in the lead aircraft during the resupply missions.

FORWARD ARMING AND REFUELING POINT PROCEDURES

7-77. Plan refueling completion before the last scheduled serial gets critically low on fuel. Other serials continue the lift operation until it is their turn to refuel. The plan should allow a smooth, continuous rotation of aircraft into and out of the FARP.

7-78. Divide the number of aircraft that can refuel at one time into the number of aircraft in the lift. The result is the number of separate trips to the FARP to refuel the entire lift one time. Multiply that result by the time required for the aircraft to refuel. The answer is the total time required to refuel one time. For example, if four serials require 15 minutes each to refuel, it takes 1 hour to refuel the entire lift. (This time includes time for repositioning to the PZ.)

7-79. To determine when in the mission to begin the refueling process, subtract the total time required to refuel one time from the available flying time. The physical planning for refueling begins when the aircraft arrive in the PZ for loading. Once the plans are developed, refueling becomes a part of the air movement table. (See FM 4-02.2 for details.)

SECTION VII – HELICOPTER CHARACTERISTICS AND PLANNING CONSIDERATIONS

7-80. The following definitions apply to the information in this section:
- **Detection** is the ability to classify a target as having military interest.
- **Recognition** is the ability to classify a target by category.
- **Identification** is the ability to determine the actual type of vehicle.
- **Infrared crossover** occurs when the emission of heat from both the target and the surrounding environment are equal, making target acquisition or detection difficult to impossible. This limitation is present in all systems that use forward-looking infrared for target acquisition.

Example. On a hot day, the ground may reflect or emit more heat than the suspected target. In this case, the environment will be "hot" and the target will be "cool." As the air cools at night, the target may lose or emit heat at a slower rate than the surrounding environment. At some point, the emission of heat from both the target and the surrounding environment may be equal. Infrared crossover occurs most often when the environment is damp or wet because the water in the air creates a buffer in the emissivity of objects.

AH-64 CHARACTERISTICS

7-81. This section addresses considerations for employment of the Longbow Apache (Table 7-2).

Table 7-2. AH-64 characteristics

Weapon Systems and Ranges	Missile range (Hellfire): 8000 m. Rocket range (Hydra 70): 6,600 to 9,000 m. Gun range (30-mm API, HEI): 4,200 m.	
Optics	**Target Acquisition and Designation System/Day Television Sensor** (low light, daytime)	**Modernized Target Acquisition Designation Sight/Forward-Looking Infrared** (day, night, weather)
	Detection: 10+ km. Recognition: 8 to 10 km. Identification: 5 to 7 km.	Detection: 10+ km. Recognition: 5 to 6 km. Identification: 90 to 1200 m (condition dependent).
Navigation Equipment	Dual embedded Global Positioning System/Inertial Navigation System, Doppler radar, and automatic direction finder.	
Flight Characteristics	Normal cruise speed: 120 kts.	
Additional Capabilities	AH-64 can be configured with an external 230-gallon fuel tank to extend its range on attack missions or with up to four 230-gallon fuel tanks for ferry or self-deployment missions.	
Limitations	Threat identification; infrared crossover; adverse weather may inhibit Hellfire engagements. (Seeker must be able to see the laser designated spot.) Overwater operations severely degrade navigation system. Pilot night vision system cannot detect wires or other small obstacles.	

OH-58 CHARACTERISTICS

7-82. This section addresses employment considerations for the Kiowa Warrior (Table 7-3).

Table 7-3. OH-58 characteristics

Weapons Systems and Ranges	Missile range (Hellfire): 8000 m. Rocket range (Hydra 70): 7000 m. Gun range (.50-caliber): 1800 m.		
Optics	Pilots use AN/AVS-6 to fly the aircraft at night.		
	Thermal Imaging System	**Television Sensor**	**Laser Range Finder/Designator**
	Detection: 10+ km. Recognition: 6 to 7 km. Identification: 3 km.	Detection: 8+ km. Recognition: 7 km. Identification: 4 to 6 km.	Maximum ranging distance: 9.99 km. Lasing a known point updates the navigation system. Maximum designating distance is limited only by thermal imaging system/television sensor.
Navigation Equipment	Embedded Global Positioning System/Inertial Navigation System in Romeo model aircraft or attitude and heading reference system. Can slave mast-mounted sight to grid input by operator.		
Flight Characteristics	Maximum speed (level): 125 kts. Normal cruise speed: 80 kts.		
Additional Capabilities	Airborne Target Handover System takes targeting data from the aircraft and transmits it digitally (secure or unsecure) to the Advanced Field Artillery Tactical Data System.		
Limitations	Threat identification; infrared crossover; adverse weather may inhibit Hellfire engagements. (Seeker must be able to see the laser designated spot.) High temperature/density altitude significantly reduces the amount of ammunition carried.		

UH-60 CHARACTERISTICS

7-83. This section addresses employment considerations for the Blackhawk helicopter (Table 7-4).

Table 7-4. UH-60 characteristics

Weapons Systems	2 X M240 (7.62-mm machine guns) for self-protection only.
Weapons Ranges	800 m (point target). 1100 m (area target).
Optics	Pilots use AN/AVS-6 to fly the aircraft at night.
Navigation Equipment	Doppler navigation set or Global Positioning System.
Flight Characteristics	Maximum speed (level): 156 kts. Normal cruise speed: 120 to 145 kts. Maximum speed (with external sling loads): 90 kts.
Additional Capabilities	External Stores Support System allows configuration for extended operations without refueling (5+ hours) (two 230-gallon fuel tanks). The External Stores Support System also allows configuration for ferry and self-deployment flights (four 230-gallon fuel tanks). Enhanced C2. Console provides the maneuver commander with an airborne platform that can support six secure VHF radios, one HF radio, two VHF radios, and two UHF radios. Volcano Mine Dispensing System, which requires 8 hours to install. UH-60 is capable of inserting and extracting troops with FRIES and SPIES.
Limitations	Using the External Stores Support System for fuel limits access to the cabin doors for troops and bulky cargo or litters. It also greatly decreases the payload. UH-60 cannot sling load a HMMWV equipped with TOW missile. Cruise speed is greatly decreased by light, bulky sling loads (less than 80 kts).

CH-47 CHARACTERISTICS

7-84. This section addresses employment considerations for the Chinook helicopter (Table 7-5).

Table 7-5. CH-47 characteristics

Weapon Systems and Ranges	3 X M240 (7.62-mm machine guns), two cabin mounted and one ramp mounted for self-protection only.
Weapons Ranges	800 m (point target). 1100 m (area target).
Optics	Pilots use AN/AVS-6 to fly the aircraft at night.
Navigation Equipment	Doppler navigation set or Global Positioning System.
Flight Characteristics	Max speed (level): 170 kts. Normal cruise speed: 120 to 145 kts.
Additional Capabilities	CH-47 can be configured with additional fuel for either mobile forward arming refueling equipment system or for ferry and self-deployment missions. CH-47 has an internal load winch to ease loading of properly configured cargo. CH-47 can sling load virtually any piece of equipment in the light Infantry, airborne, or air assault divisions.
Limitations	Cruise speed is greatly decreased by light, bulky sling loads (less than 80 kts).

CH-46 CHARACTERISTICS

7-85. This section addresses employment considerations for the CH-46 Sea Knight helicopter (Table 7-6).

Table 7-6. CH-46E characteristics

Weapon Systems	2 X .50-caliber XM 218.	
Weapons Range	1800 m.	
Navigation Equipment	Global Positioning System.	Miniature Airborne GPS Receiver System.
Communication Equipment	VHF/UHF.	12 X AN/ARC-210 w/KY-58 encryption device (CNCS configured aircraft only).
Flight Characteristics	Maximum airspeed: 145 knots indicated air speed (KIAS).	Payloads: 4300 lbs/12 passengers.
	Maximum endurance: 70 KIAS.	Endurance: 2 hours 55 minutes.
	Maximum range: 110 to 130 KIAS.	
Aircraft Survivability Equipment	Radar warning receiver.	AN/APR-39(V)1 radar warning receiver.
	Infrared countermeasures.	AN/ALQ-157 infrared jammer.
	Expendables.	AN/ALE-39 countermeasures dispenser.
	Missile warning.	AN/AAR-47 missile warning system.
Fuel Capacity	4488 lbs/660 gallons.	

CH-53 CHARACTERISTICS

7-86. This section addresses employment considerations for the CH-53D Sea Stallion and CH-53E Super Stallion helicopter (Table 7-7 and Table 7-8).

Table 7-7. CH-53D characteristics

Weapon Systems	2 X .50-caliber XM 218.	
Weapons Range	1800 m.	
Communication Equipment	HF.	1 X AN/ARC-94 or AN/ ARC-174.
	Ultrahigh frequency/Very high frequency.	2 X AN/ARC-182 with KY- 58 encryption device or 2 X AN/ARC-210 with KY- 58 encryption device.
Flight Characteristics	Maximum endurance: 70 KIAS.	Payload: 37 passengers/8,000 lbs internal.
	Maximum airspeed: 130 KIAS.	Typical: 3 + 00 hours.
		Best Case: 5 + 30 hours.
Aircraft Survivability Equipment	Radar warning receiver.	AN/APR-39(V)1 radar warning receiver.
	Infrared countermeasures.	AN/ALQ-157.
	Missile warning.	AN/AAR-47 missile warning system.
Fuel Capacity	13,178 lbs/1,938 gallons.	

Table 7-8. CH-53E characteristics

Weapon Systems	2 X .50-caliber XM 218.	
Weapons Range	1800 m.	
Communication Equipment	High frequency.	1 X AN/ARC-94 or AN/ ARC-174.
	Ultrahigh frequency/Very high frequency.	2 X AN/ARC-182 with KY- 58 encryption device or 2 X AN/ARC-210 with KY- 58 encryption device.
Flight Characteristics	Normal cruise airspeed: 135 KIAS.	Payload: 37–55 passengers/20,000 lbs internal.
		Typical: 4 + 00 hours.
	Maximum airspeed: 150 KIAS.	Best Case: Indefinite with aerial refueling.
Aircraft Survivability Equipment	Radar warning receiver.	AN/APR-39(V)1 radar warning receiver.
	Infrared countermeasures.	None.
	Missile warning.	AN/AAR-47 missile warning system.
Fuel Capacity	15,000 lbs/2,277 gallons.	
Other systems	Forward-looking infrared.	AN/AAQ-16B.

MV-22B CHARACTERISTICS

7-87. This section addresses employment considerations for the MV-22 Osprey aircraft (Table 7-9).

Table 7-9. MV-22B characteristics

Weapons Systems and Ranges	M240 (7.62-mm machine gun): 800 m (point target) and 1,100 m (area target).	
	M2 (.50-caliber machine gun): 1,800 m.	
	Remote Guardian System GAU-17 minigun (7.62-mm): 1,000 m.	
Communication Equipment	Internal.	AN/AIC-30.
	External.	ARC-210 radio.
Navigation Equipment	Navigational aid.	ARN-147.
Flight Characteristics	Cruise airspeed: 240 kts.	Payload: 24 passengers/20,000 lbs internal or 15,000 lbs of external cargo (with dual hooks).
	Max airspeed: 250 kts (at sea level) and 305 kts (at 15,000 ft).	Endurance: 200 nautical miles with troops.
Aircraft Survivability Equipment	RWR.	AN/APR-39A(V)2.
	Laser warning.	AN/AVR-2A Laser Detection System.
	Missile warning.	AN/AAR-47.
	Electronic countermeasures.	ALE-47 Countermeasures Dispensing System.
Fuel Capacity	1,448 gallons/9,850 lbs.	
Other capabilities	Self deployable, vertical/short takeoff and landing.	

MI-17 (MI 8) CHARACTERISTICS

7-88. This section addresses employment considerations for the MI-17 (MI-8M) Hip (Table 7-10).

Table 7-10. MI-17 (MI-8M)

Weapons Systems and Ranges	Six external hardpoints, capable of mounting various missiles, bombs, small arms, and cannons (mission dictated).
	2x 7.62-mm or 1x 12.7-mm machine gun: approx 800 m or approx 1500 m.
	4-6 - AT-2C or AT-3 ATGM: 2500 m or 3000 m.
	4-6 – 57-mm rocket pods (16 each).
	2 – 80-mm rocket pods (20 each).
	4 – 250-kg bombs.
	2 – 500-kg bombs.
	1 - 12.7-mm machine gun pod: approx 1500 m.
	2 - Twin 23-mm gun pods: approx 2000 m.
	Most probable armament: fitted with 2x 7.62-mm machine guns or possibly 2x 23-mm GSh-23 gun packs in cabin, 57-mm rockets, and AT3/SAGGER ATGM.
Navigation Equipment	Doppler Radar and a fully functioning autopilot.
Flight Characteristics	Cruise airspeed: 230 kts. Payload: 24 Passengers/4000 kg internal or 3000 kg external on sling only.
	Max airspeed: 300 kts. Range: 495 km (1065 km with aux fuel).
Aircraft Survivability	Main and tail rotors electrically deiced.
	Infrared jammer.
	Chaff and flares.
	Armor plating.
	Exhaust diffusers.
Fuel Capacity	Internal: 445 liters.
	Internal Aux Tank: 915 liters each.
	External Fuel Tank (Port): 745 liters.
	External Fuel Tank (Starboard): 680 liters.
Other Capabilities	Single engine flight in the event of loss of power by one engine.

TYPICAL FUEL EXPENDITURE RATES AND CAPACITIES

7-89. Table 7-11 depicts typical rates of fuel expenditures per helicopter and fuel capacities without additional tanks.

Table 7-11. Typical helicopter fuel expenditure rates and capacities

Helicopter	Average Gallons Per Hour	Fuel Capacity
AH-64	175	370
OH-58	44	112
OH-58 (armed)	110	112
UH-60	178	362
CH-47	514	1,030

STANDARD LOAD CAPACITIES

7-90. The ADAM/BAE should have a copy of the standard operator manuals for each type of helicopter. Although aircraft may be capable of carrying more than is indicated on these lists, safety, loading procedures, space limitations, and other factors dictate authorized loads for each helicopter. Environmental conditions and configuration constraints affect the ACL load for each aircraft. This information must be updated and obtained from each unit either periodically or when there is an obvious change. (See Table 7-12 and Table 7-13 for load capacities and planning weights.)

Table 7-12. Typical helicopter load capacities

Type	Empty Weight Plus Crew and Fuel	Max Gross Weight	Max Sling Load
UH-60A	14,000 lbs	22,000 lbs	8,000 lbs
UH-60L	14,250 lbs	23,000 lbs	9,000 lbs
CH-47D	30,000 lbs	50,000 lbs	26,000 lbs

Table 7-13. Typical planning weights for combat equipment and vehicles

Vehicle/Equipment	Weight in Pounds
M998 HMMWV	7,535
M996 HMMWV TOW Missile Carrier	8,095
M149 Water Buffalo	2,540 (empty) 6,060 (loaded)
M101A1 trailer, ¾ ton	1,350 (empty) 2,850 (loaded)
500-gallon fuel drum	275 (empty) 3,625 (full)
M102 105-mm Howitzer	3,360
M119 105-mm Howitzer	4,000
M198 155-mm Howitzer	15,740
A22 bag	2,200 (loaded)
Conex steel aluminum	6,500 (max load) 2,140 (empty) 1,560 (empty)
Scamp crane	14,600
One mil-van	4,710
Electronic shop with wheels	3,940
Tool set, shop with wheels	3,030
Shop, portable, aircraft maintenance	4,220 (empty) 5,425 (loaded)
M1008 pickup	5,900 (empty) 8,800 (loaded)
JD-550 Dozer	16,800

ATTACK RECONNAISSANCE AIRCRAFT MUNITIONS LOADS

7-91. As with the assault and general support aviation battalion helicopter units, the BAO must coordinate with attack reconnaissance helicopter units to determine standard munitions and fuel loads for those types of assets. Factors such as weather, temperature, and elevation all affect the maximum ordnance loads. (See Table 7-14 for typical attack reconnaissance helicopter maximum ordnance loads.)

Table 7-14. Typical attack reconnaissance helicopter maximum ordnance loads

Aircraft	Gun	2.75-Inch Rockets	Missiles
AH-64 (Standard)	1,200	38	8 Hellfire
AH-64 (Heavy)	1,200		16 Hellfire
OH-58D	500	14	4 Hellfire

Glossary

Acronym/Terms	Definition
AATF	air assault task force
AATFC	air assault task force commander
ABCS	Army Battle Command System
ABN	air battle net
AC2	airspace command and control
ACL	allowable cargo load
ACO	airspace control order
ADAM	air defense airspace management
ALO	air liaison officer
AMB	air mission brief
AMC	air mission commander
AMCM	air mission coordination meeting
AMPS	Aviation Mission Planning System
AO	area of operations
AVN LNO	aviation liaison officer
BAE	brigade aviation element
BAO	brigade aviation officer
BCT	brigade combat team
BDA	battle damage assessment
BFT	blue force tracker
BSB	brigade support battalion
C2	command and control
CAB	combat aviation brigade
CAN	combat aviation net
CBRN	chemical, biological, radiological, and nuclear
CCA	close combat attack
CNR	combat net radio
CP	command post
EPLRS	Enhanced Position Location Reporting System
FARP	forward arming and refueling point
FBCB2	Force XXI Battle Command, Brigade and Below
FS	fire support
FSO	fire support officer
FRIES	Fast-Insertion/Extraction System
GTC	ground tactical commander
HBCT	heavy brigade combat team
HF	high frequency
HMMWV	high-mobility multipurpose wheeled vehicle
IPC	initial planning conference
JTAC	joint terminal attack controller
LZ	landing zone
MDMP	military decision-making process

MEDEVAC	medical evacuation
METT-TC	mission, enemy, terrain and weather, troops and support available, time available, and civil considerations
OE	operational environment
OPCON	operational control
PZ	pickup zone
PZCO	pickup zone control officer
RDSP	rapid decision-making and synchronization process
ROZ	restricted operations zone
RP	release point
S-1	personnel staff officer
S-2	intelligence staff officer
S-3	operations staff officer
S-4	logistics staff officer
S-6	command, control, communications, and computer operations officer
SBCT	Stryker brigade combat team
SEAD	suppression of enemy air defenses
SP	start point
SPIES	Special Patrol Insertion/Extraction System
SPO	support operations officer
TOW	tube-launched, optically-tracked, wire-guided
UAS	unmanned aircraft systems
UHF	ultrahigh frequency
VHF	very high frequency

References

SOURCES USED
These are the sources quoted or paraphrased in this publication.

FIELD MANUALS
FM 1-02, *Operational Terms and Graphics*, 21 September 2004.

FM 3-0, *Operations*, 27 February 2008.

FM 3-52, *Army Airspace Command and Control in a Combat Zone*, 1 August 2002.

FM 3-90, *Tactics*, 4 July 2001.

FM 4-20.197, *Multiservice Helicopter Sling Load: Basic Operations and Equipment*, 20 July 2006.

FM 6-0, *Mission Command: Command and Control of Army Forces*, 11 August 2003.

FM 7-0, *Training Units and Developing Leaders for Full Spectrum Operation*, 23 February 2011.

JOINT PUBLICATIONS
JP 1-02, *Department of Defense Dictionary of Military and Associated Terms*, 30 September 2010.

JP 3-0, *Joint Operations,* 22 March 2010.

JP 3-18, *Joint Forcible Entry Operations*, 16 June 2008.

JP 3-52, *Joint Airspace Control,* 20 May 2010.

JP 5-0, *Joint Operation Planning*, 26 December 2006.

DOCUMENTS NEEDED
These documents must be available to the intended user of this publication.

DA FORMS
DA forms are available on the APD Web site (www.apd.army.mil).

DA Form 2028, *Recommended Changes to Publications and Blank Forms*

DA Form 7382, *Sling Load Inspection Record.*

ARMY REGULATIONS
AR 95-1, *Flight Regulations*, 12 November 2008.

FIELD MANUALS
FM 2-01.3, *Intelligence Preparation of the Battlefield/Battlespace*, 15 October 2009.

FM 3-04.111, *Aviation Brigades*, 7 December 2007.

FM 3-04.113, *Utility and Cargo Helicopter Operations*, 7 December 2007.

FM 3-04.126, *Attack Reconnaissance Helicopter Operations,* 16 February 2007.

FM 3-04.155, *Army Unmanned Aircraft System Operations*, 29 July 2009.

FM 3-05.210, *Special Forces Air Operations*, 27 February 2009.

FM 3-09.32, *Multi-Service Tactics, Techniques, and Procedures for the Joint Application of Firepower*, 20 December 2007.

FM 3-20.96, *Reconnaissance and Cavalry Squadron*, 12 March 2010.

FM 3-21.38, *Pathfinder Operations*, 25 April 2006.

FM 3-37, *Protection,* 30 September 2009.

FM 3-60, *The Targeting Process*, 26 November 2010.

FM 3-90.6, *Brigade Combat Team,* 14 September 2010.

FM 4-02.2, *Medical Evacuation*, 8 May 2007.

FM 5-0, *The Operations Process*, 26 March 2010.

FM 5-19, *Composite Risk Management*, 21 August 2006.

FM 6-01.1, *Knowledge Management Section*, 29 August 2008.

FM 6-02.53, *Tactical Radio Operations*, 5 August 2009.

JOINT PUBLICATIONS

JP 3-01, *Countering Air and Missile Threats*, 22 March 2010.

JP 3-09.3, *Close Air Support*, 8 July 2009. *Countering Air and Missile Threats*, 22 March 2010.

TRAINING CIRCULARS

TC 2-01, *Intelligence, Surveillance, and Reconnaissance Synchronization*, 22 September 2010.

RECOMMENDED READING

These sources contain relevant supplemental information.

FIELD MANUALS

FM 3-04.104, *Tactics, Techniques, and Procedures for Forward Arming and Refueling Point*, 3 August 2006.

FM 3-20.971, *Reconnaissance and Cavalry Troop*, 4 August 2009.

FM 3-21.8, *The Infantry Platoon and Squad*, 28 March 2007.

TRAINING CIRCULARS

TC 1-400, *Brigade Aviation Element Handbook*, 27 April 2006.

Index

This page intentionally left blank.

By order of the Secretary of the Army:

GEORGE W. CASEY, JR.
General, United States Army
Chief of Staff

Official:

JOYCE E. MORROW
Administrative Assistant to the
Secretary of the Army
1103901

DISTRIBUTION:

Active Army, Army National Guard, and U.S. Army Reserve: To be distributed in accordance with the initial distribution number (IDN) 110400, requirements for ATTP 3-18.12.

www.ingramcontent.com/pod-product-compliance
Lightning Source LLC
Chambersburg PA
CBHW080208300326
41934CB00038B/3405